THE
COMPACT
HANDBOOK
OF
OLD TESTAMENT
LIFE

THE COMPACT

OF

OLD TESTAMENT

LIFE

BETHANY HOUSE PUBLISHERS
MINNEAPOLIS, MINNESOTA 55438
A Division of Bethany Fellowship, Inc.

Originally titled *The World of the Old Testament* and published in Great Britain by Scripture Union, 130 City Road, London EC1V 2NJ.

Maps by Neil Pinchbeck.

Published by Bethany House Publishers
A Division of Bethany Fellowship, Inc.
6820 Auto Club Road, Minneapolis, Minnesota 55438

Printed in the United States of America

Library of Congress Cataloging-in-Publication Data

Bimson, John J.
    The compact handbook of Old Testament life / John Bimson.
        p.   cm.

    1. Sociology, Biblical. 2. Bible. O.T.—Criticism, interpretation, etc.
I. Title.
BS1199.S6B55   1988
221.9'5—dc19   88–18750
ISBN 1-55661-046-7   CIP

To My Wife
Maya

JOHN BIMSON is the Librarian and Lecturer in Old Testament and Hebrew at Trinity College, Bristol, England. He obtained a BA and PhD in Biblical Studies at Sheffield University, specializing in Old Testament history and archeology. He is the author of *Redating the Exodus and Conquest*, co-author of *The New Bible Atlas*, and a contributer to *Essays on the Patriarchal Narratives* as well as various other publications.

Contents

Palestine

showing major towns, physical features and main routes

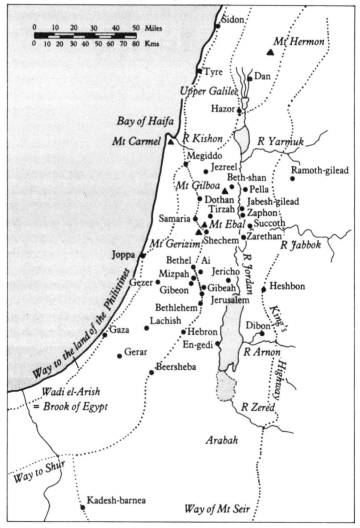

CHAPTER ONE

The Land

Geographically, the world of the Old Testament was much larger than the land of Palestine. Abraham, the ancestor of the nation of Israel, was called by God from Ur in southern Mesopotamia; later the Israelite tribes descended from him spent over four centuries in Egypt; much later still, the tribe of Judah was in exile in Babylon for almost fifty years (and thus the nation returned to its geographical starting-point). After the Babylonian Exile not all Jews returned to their 'promised land', and the book of Esther (and the opening chapter of Nehemiah) is set in Susa, capital of the Persian empire. Indeed, by the time of Esther (fifth century BC), there were Jews scattered throughout the Persian empire, 'from India to Ethiopia' (Est 8:9). Nevertheless, Palestine plays a uniquely important role in the Old Testament story, and it is with a survey of this land and its character that we begin.

The names of the land and its people

Israel's 'promised land' has had a bewildering variety of names during the last 4000 years, and some explanation of them may be helpful.

The oldest name used for the land in the Old Testament is 'Canaan', a term which occurs most frequently in Genesis–Judges. Originally it applied to the land and inhabitants of the coastal plains of Syria-Palestine. Hence in Numbers 13:29, Joshua 5:1; 11:3 etc, the Canaanites are associated with the coast, the valleys and plains, while Amorites and other groups are placed in the hills. However, it was also used less strictly to include the whole hinterland as far east as the Jordan (eg Num 13:17–21; 34:2–12). These wider and narrower uses are both found in ancient texts outside the Bible, as well as in the Old Testament.

Some time during the period known as the Late Bronze Age (about 1500–1200 BC) the Israelites entered Canaan under Joshua. (See ch 2 for a discussion of possible dates within that period.) Their conquest of the land was followed in the twelfth century BC by an influx of Philistines from either Crete or Cyprus. The main area of Philistine settlement was the southern coastal plain. These invasions largely restricted the original Canaanites to Phoenicia (see 2 Sam 24:7). Some Canaanites remained in cities within Israel's territory (eg 1 Kings 9:16), but the term 'Canaan' as a name for the land seems to have dropped out of use after the time of the judges (though see Zeph 2:5 for an instance of its use in the seventh century BC).

The term 'Palestine' is derived from the Philistines. In the fifth century BC the Greek historian Herodotus seems to have used the term *Palaistine Syria* (= Philistine Syria) to refer to the whole region between Phoenicia and the Lebanon mountains in the north and Egypt in the south. (While the exact meaning intended by Herodotus is debated, later Greek writers certainly used 'Philistine Syria' in this very broad sense.) During the second century BC, under the Hasmonean priest-kings, the name of the tribe of Judah became applied to a very wide region, and when the Romans took control of that territory in 63 BC they called it *Provincia Judaea*. However, in AD 135, after putting down the second major Jewish revolt against Rome, the Emperor Hadrian wanted to blot out the name 'Judah' completely. He therefore changed the name of the province to *Provincia Syria Palaestina* (ie the Latin version of the Greek term). This was later shortened to *Palaestina*, from which the modern 'Palestine' is derived. Since the term does not originate until the fifth century BC at the earliest, it does not occur in the Old

Testament. (In the KJV we do find 'Palestine' in Joel 3:4 and 'Palestina' in Exod 15:14 and Isa 14:29, but these are errors of translation; both should be 'Philistia', as in the RSV.)

Today the name 'Palestine' has political overtones which many find objectionable, and for that reason some writers deliberately avoid using it. However, the alternatives are either too clumsy to be used repeatedly, or else they are inaccurate when applied to certain periods, so 'Palestine' remains a useful term when kept free of political implications, and will be used frequently in this book.

From the emergence of an Israelite state under Saul, we find the land called 'the land of Israel' (eg 1 Sam 13:19; 2 Kings 5:2; 2 Chron 34:7; Ezek 7:2 etc). This should not be understood to mean 'the land *called* Israel', for in the Old Testament period 'Israel' was first and foremost the name of a *people*. It therefore means 'the land of [the people] Israel'. However, 'Israel' also had a secondary and more restricted meaning; it was sometimes used as a name for the northern tribes (as distinct from Judah), and when the kingdom divided after the death of Solomon (1 Kings 12), 'Israel' became the name of the independent northern state.

The term 'promised land' refers, of course, to God's promise to give the land of Canaan to Abraham's descendants (Gen 13:14–15; 15:18–21; 17:8). The expression 'the Holy Land' has its origin in Zechariah 2:12, but did not become a common designation for the land until the Middle Ages. The land is, of course, no longer holy to the Jews alone, but also to Christians and Muslims.

It may also be useful to mention the correct use of names for the *people* to whom the land was given by God. If we follow biblical precedent, it is certainly correct to call them 'Hebrews' from Abraham onwards (see Gen 14:13). The origin and scope of this name is very much debated among Old Testament scholars, but the Old Testament itself implies some connection with Eber, Abraham's ancestor (Gen 10:21–31; 11:14–26). 'Israel' was the new name given by God to Jacob, Abraham's grandson (Gen 32:28; 43:6, etc), and so the descendants of Jacob are 'Israelites' or, collectively, 'Israel'. In Exodus 3:18 and 5:1–3 'Hebrews' and 'Israel' appear to be used as synonymous terms (though if 'Hebrews' indicates the descendants of Eber, then Hebrews were, strictly speaking, a much wider group than the tribes of Israel). As already mentioned, 'Israel' also has a secondary and more specific meaning in the Old Testament, since it can signify the northern tribes as distinct from Judah, especially after the division of the kingdom.

Although the terms 'Hebrew' and 'Israelite' continued in use into the New Testament period (eg Rom 9:4; 2 Cor 11:22; Phil 3:5), by then the term 'Jew' was more commonly used. This originally referred to a member of the southern tribe of Judah (which is its use in Jer 32:12; 34:9), but after the Babylonian Exile it came to replace 'Israelite' as the most widely-used term for one of God's covenant people. This was because, by that time, virtually all Israelites were in fact members of the tribe of Judah, as the northern tribes ('Israel' in the narrow sense) had lost their identity after the fall of Samaria in 722 BC (see ch 2). The exceptions were chiefly members of the tribe of Benjamin (Ezra 1:5; Phil 3:5), which had been linked with Judah since the division of the kingdom. 'Jew' and 'Jewish' should not be used in the generally accepted sense when speaking of the period before the Exile.

The extent of Israel's territory

It is difficult to be precise about the limits of Israel's territory, because different biblical texts define them in different ways. In a number of texts (Num 34:5; Josh 15:4, 47, etc) the southern limit of the land given to the Israelite tribes is 'the Brook of Egypt'. This is the Wadi el-Arish, a seasonal stream which flows from northern Sinai into the Mediterranean about eighty kilometres west of Gaza. However, south of Beersheba the land is not very suitable for cultivation and settlement, so Beersheba became the effective southern boundary, and is mentioned as such in a number of passages (referred to below). The eastern boundary is defined by the river Jordan (Num 34:10–12), though Moses allowed the tribes of Reuben, Gad and half the tribe of Manasseh to settle east of the Jordan (Num 32; Josh 22). It would seem from other passages, however, that their hold on this Transjordanian territory was rather precarious, since we find Ammonites, Moabites and others dominating the area in later centuries. The western boundary was ideally the coast of the Mediterranean, which the Old Testament calls 'the Great Sea' (Num 34:6), but the southern coastal plain became Philistine territory from the twelfth century BC onwards, so the ideal was never realized.

The northern boundary as defined in Numbers 34: 7–9 likewise never became a reality. This passage places it as far north as 'the entrance of Hamath' (or 'Lebo Hamath') in present-day Syria, but the land actually occupied by the Israelites never extended this far. Genesis 15: 18 and Joshua 1: 4 speak of an even more northerly limit, namely the Euphrates. While the people of Israel never *occupied* such a vast region, the area conquered by David extended towards Hamath (2 Sam 8: 3–10), and Solomon incorporated Hamath itself into his empire (2 Chron 8: 3–4). Indeed, because certain states in the north were vassals of David and Solomon, their empire could be described as extending to the Euphrates (2 Chron 9: 26). It should be stressed, however, that this was *foreign* territory ruled by the empire at its height, not *Israelite* territory.

The effective territory of 'all Israel' is said in many Old Testament passages to extend from Dan in the north to Beersheba in the south (eg Judg 20: 1; 1 Sam 3: 20; 2 Sam 3: 10; 1 Kings 4: 25, etc). Indeed, the phrase 'from Dan to Beersheba' seems to have been a traditional one, equivalent to our 'from Land's End to John O'Groats'. In our survey of Palestine (below), Dan and Beersheba will be the northern and southern limits adopted.

The area between these limits, and between the Mediterranean coast and the Jordan valley, is about the size of Wales. It is a striking thought that so many significant events should have taken place in this relatively small area. As we will see in chapter 2, the country owed much of its importance to its strategic position as a land-bridge and buffer-zone between Europe, Asia and Africa.

Climate

For a small country, Palestine contains a surprising variety of climatic conditions. Probably no other region of similar size can boast so many contrasts. To the east of Dan lies Mount Hermon, a range of mountains rising to 3030 metres (9200 feet). Here a covering of snow remains all through the summer months. Only 185 kilometres (125 miles) to the south lies the Dead Sea, the surface of which is some 400 metres (1300 feet) *below* sea-level, and where the daytime summer temperature is a stifling 40° C (104 F).

There are major temperature changes between daytime and nightime, and also considerable variation between different areas of the country. To illustrate this point, the following table shows the summer temperature variation for the three main regions between the coast and the Jordan.

Coastal plain	day	29 C	(84.2 F)
	night	23 C	(73.4 F)
Central hills	day	30 C	(86 F)
	night	18 C	(64.4 F)
Jordan valley	day	39 C	(102.2 F)
	night	23 C	(73.4 F)

The short distances between these regions serve to highlight the variation. At the latitude of Jerusalem it is only about fifty-five kilometres (thirty-six miles) from the coast to the highest elevations of the central hills (1000 metres, or 3280 feet), and only another thirty-six kilometres (twenty-four miles) from there to the Jordan.

There are also striking contrasts between summer and winter. For comparison with the temperatures given above, here are the average temperatures for January, the coldest month of the winter.

Coastal plain	day	17 C	(62.6 F)
	night	9 C	(48.2 F)
Central hills	day	13 C	(55.4 F)
	night	5 C	(41 F)
Jordan valley	day	20 C	(68 F)
	night	10 C	(50 F)

On some winter nights the temperature in the central hills is low enough to cause heavy falls of snow. The snow rarely lasts long, however, as the daytime temperature is always above freezing. The Old Testament thinks it worthy of record that Benaiah, the chief of David's bodyguard, 'slew a lion in a pit on a day when snow had fallen' (2 Sam 23:20).

In Palestine the difference between summer and winter is not just one of temperature, for winter is the rainy season. This begins in October and lasts until April, the heaviest rainfall coming around the middle of the period. As with temperatures, the rainfall varies from one region to another. Southwesterly winds predominate during the rainy season, so rainfall tends to be heaviest in the north and west, becoming lighter toward the south and east. Higher regions also receive more rain than lower ones. The heaviest rainfall is in Upper Galilee, where the annual average is 1000 mm (40 inches); Jerusalem gets an average of 560 mm (24 inches); around the Dead Sea the annual total is less than 50 mm (2 inches). It is worth noticing that Jerusalem's average is *about the same as London's!* The big difference, however, is that Jerusalem receives its rainfall in a total of about 50 days, and most of those are concentrated in the months of December, January and February. But even in winter Palestine has more sunny days than rainy ones.

The rainy season often begins with thunderstorms, caused by moist sea air encountering hot, dry air rising from the land. At this time, early in October, the rain is unevenly distributed. Mid- or late October brings the really effective rains from the farmer's point of view, referred to in the Old Testament as the 'former (or early) rains' (Joel 2:23). The onset of the autumn rains may be dramatic and violent, damaging homes and causing sudden torrents which can sweep people away (Judg 5:21). But in Old Testament times they were vital to the success of the wheat and barley harvests, and so their arrival was longed for and rejoiced in (Ps 65:9–13). The first rains of the season broke up the hard earth and prepared the land for ploughing and sowing. The last showers of the season, in April, are referred to as the 'latter rains' (Joel 2:23). It was important that the rain persisted right through to this time, or the grain harvest (in May) would fail (Amos 4:7–8).

The end of the rainy season also brought the warmer temperatures of summer. Hence the Song of Solomon declares: 'Lo, the winter is past, the rain is over and gone' (2:11). But while early summer is a pleasant season (Song of Sol 2:12–13), it is also the beginning of five or six months (usually May–Oct) when no rain falls at all. This hot, dry period sees parts of the land turn from green to brown as low vegetation disappears. By the end of May the new grass and the multitude of flowers which appear in winter and spring (lilies, cyclamen, narcissi, anemones and orchids) have mostly gone. By August many areas are thoroughly parched and

11

dusty. Hence the psalmist can say: 'my strength was dried up as by the heat of summer' (32:4). Apart from human efforts at water storage and irrigation, crops growing during these months are dependent on the heavy dew which falls during the summer nights.

The farming year

On the eve of their entry into the 'promised land', Moses described it to the Israelites as 'a land of wheat and barley, of vines and fig trees and pomegranates, a land of olive trees and honey, a land in which you will eat bread without scarcity, in which you will lack nothing . . .' (Deut 8:8–9). This by no means exhausts the list of Palestine's produce in ancient times. We find 'balm . . . honey, gum, myrrh, pistachio nuts and almonds' described by Jacob as 'some of the choice fruits of the land' (Gen 43:11). In the twentieth century BC, a hundred years or so before Jacob's time, an Egyptian called Sinuhe spent several years in exile in northern Palestine, and his description of his experiences (*The Tale of Sinuhe*) includes a vivid picture of the land's richness. It is worth setting this alongside Moses' description of the land quoted above.

> Figs were in it, and grapes. It had more wine than water. Plentiful was its honey, abundant its olives. Every kind of fruit was on its trees. Barley was there, and emmer wheat. There was no limit to any kind of cattle. . . . Bread was made for me as daily fare, wine as daily provision, cooked meat and roast fowl . . . and milk in every kind of cooking.

Sheep and goats were raised for their milk and meat, and sheep also provided wool for clothing. Goat's hair was also woven into coarse cloth, and the skins of goats, with all the hair removed, were used to make containers for water, milk and wine (Josh 9:13, 1 Sam 25:18, etc). Rich farmers kept enormous flocks; Nabal had 3000 sheep and 1000 goats (1 Sam 25:2). Cattle were also kept (Gen 12:16; Num 7:6–8; 1 Sam 22:19, and see Sinuhe, quoted above), though not all areas were suitable for them. As well as providing meat, oxen were used as draught animals, pulling carts and ploughs and turning machinery such as olive-presses (see ch 4). Agriculture and pastoralism were complementary pursuits. Sheep

12

and goats were grazed in the highland areas during the winter months, when grass was plentiful. During the summer they were brought to the lowlands to graze among the stubble of the harvested fields, which they also fertilized for the next season.

The rhythm of the farming year is portrayed for us in a short Hebrew inscription from about the time of Solomon (tenth century BC). This occurs on a piece of limestone discovered during excavations at Gezer in 1908, and seems to be a child's ditty, perhaps a memory-verse like our 'Thirty days hath September . . .'. It groups the twelve months of the farmer's year as follows:

> His two months are olive harvest,
> his two months are planting grain,
> his two months are late planting;
> his month is hoeing up flax,
> his month is barley harvest,
> his month is wheat harvest and [feasting?];
> his two months are vine-tending,
> his month is summer fruit.

The Gezer calendar, a Hebrew inscription of the tenth century BC, detailing the farming year.

In the following paragraphs we will relate this to the months of our year, adding biblical references where appropriate.

The olive harvest can begin as early as September, when the olives begin to fall from the trees, but is not usually over until mid-November. In Old Testament times the olives were shaken from the trees by beating the branches with sticks (Isa 17:6).

Wheat and barley were sown following the autumn rains in late October and November (and so overlapped the olive harvest; the child's rhyme separates activities which actually ran into each other). Because the tasks of ploughing and sowing were hard work, and the final yield uncertain, the Old Testament draws a stark contrast between this time and the joy of harvest (Ps 126:5). The seed was sometimes scattered broadcast from a basket (as in the New Testament parable of the sower, Luke 8:5–8), but some farmers planted their wheat in rows in the furrows (Isa 28:25).

The 'late planting' refers to the sowing of a variety of crops (eg millet, lentils, chick-peas, onions, leeks, garlic and cucumbers), which took place from mid-January to mid-March. It is also referred to in Amos 7:1 ('the second crop', NIV; 'the latter growth', RSV). Between sowing and harvest the crops were exposed to a variety of hazards, including hailstorms (Hag 2:17), blight and mildew (Deut 28:22; Amos 4:9), the growth of weeds such as thistles and thorns (Jer 12:13), the browsing of sheep or cattle (Exod 22:5) and a failure of the 'latter rains' (Amos 4:7).

Flax, from which linen was obtained for clothing, was harvested in March–April (Josh 2:6), barley in April–May and wheat in May–June. These are only approximate dates, however, as the exact time of harvest depended on the weather and on local conditions, especially altitude. The barley harvest, for example, would have begun in mid-April around Jericho, which lies in the Jordan valley; it would have started about ten days later on the coastal plain, and as much as a month later in upland areas. The grain crops were harvested with sickles, cutting the stalk not far below the head (Job 24:24; Isa 17:5). Enough stalk was attached for the harvested grain to be bound into sheaves (Gen 37:7), but these were not tall and upstanding like those traditional on English farms until recent years. The barley and wheat harvests together were reckoned to last seven weeks, and culminated in the 'Feast of Weeks', a harvest festival marked by great rejoicing (Lev 23:15–21; Deut 16:9–12).

The vines were pruned between mid-June and mid-August, and

	Month	Pre-exilic name	Post-exilic name	Modern equivalent	Season	Festivals
Rain	1	ABIB Exod 13:4; 23:15; 34:18; Deut 16:1	NISAN Est 3:7 Neh 2:1	Mar-Apr	Spring Latter rains Flax harvest	14 Passover (Exod 12:18; Lev 23:5) 15-21 Unleavened Bread (Lev 23:6) 16 Firstfruits (Lev 23:10f.)
Dry	2	ZIV 1 Kings 6:1, 37	IYYAR	Apr-May	Barley harvest Dry season begins	14 Later Passover (Num 9:10-11)
	3		SIVAN Est 8:9	May-June	Early figs ripen Wheat harvest	6 Pentecost (Lev 23:15ff.) Feast of Weeks Harvest
	4		TAMMUZ	June-July	Vine tending	
	5		AB	July-Aug	Grape harvest	
	6		ELUL Neh 6:15	Aug-Sept	Olive harvest Dates and summer figs	
Rain	7	ETHANIM 1 Kings 8:2	TISHRI	Sept-Oct	Early rains	1 Trumpets (Num 29:1; Lev 23:24) 10 Day of Atonement (Lev 16:29ff.; 23:27ff.) 15-21 Tabernacles (Lev 23:34 ff.) 22 Solemn assembly (Lev 23:36)
	8	BUL 1 Kings 6:38	MARCHESVAN	Oct-Nov	Ploughing Winter figs	
	9		CHISLEV Neh 1:1	Nov-Dec	Sowing	25 Dedication (1 Macc 4:52f.; John 10:22)
Cold	10		TEBETH Est 2:16	Dec-Jan	Rains (snow on high ground)	
	11		SHEBAT Zech 1:7	Jan-Feb	Almond blossom	
Rain	12		ADAR Est 3:7	Feb-Mar	Citrus fruit harvest	

The Hebrew calendar, showing seasons and festivals with modern equivalents.

15

the grapes gathered in August–September (though in low-lying districts the harvest began as early as July). This was also the season for the gathering of dates, figs and pomegranates, ie the 'summer fruit' (an expression also used in Amos 8:2). Traditionally this was another period of rejoicing and festival (Judg 9:27; Isa 16:10), which found religious expression in the 'Feast of Booths' (Lev 23:33–36; Deut 16:13–15).

Of the various crops mentioned here, the three most important in Old Testament times were clearly grain (from which bread was made), grapes (which provided wine – and also raisins, 1 Sam 25:18, etc) and olives (which provided olive oil, used for cooking and lighting). Hence grain, wine and oil are frequently mentioned in the Old Testament (eg Deut 33:28; 1 Kings 5:11; 2 Chron 2:15; Ezek 16:19; 27:17; Hos 2:8, etc). These were the three staple products and the basis of Palestine's agricultural economy.

We see from the above outline of the agricultural year that it was both demanding and uncertain in its outcome. The farmers of ancient Israel did not have an easy time, in spite of the fertility of the land and the wide variety of its produce. From October to April the farmer was busy ploughing, sowing and weeding; from April he was occupied with reaping, threshing and storing the grain. The spring harvest was followed by work in the orchards and vineyards, culminating in the autumn harvest. The lives of all who lived in the land were tied to the rhythm of the seasons, because all were ultimately dependent on the outcome of the harvests, and because the great religious festivals also reflected the agricultural year.

The geography of Palestine

In describing the geography of Palestine it is convenient to divide the country into a number of parallel strips running from north to south. As we saw above when comparing local temperatures, between the coast and the Jordan there are three main 'strips': the coastal plain, the central hill country and the Jordan valley. Here we will also include a fourth, namely the highlands to the east of the Jordan valley. In describing the southern half of the country it is necessary to introduce two subdivisions: the Shephelah (between the coastal plain and the hill country) and the Judean desert

Physical regions of Palestine

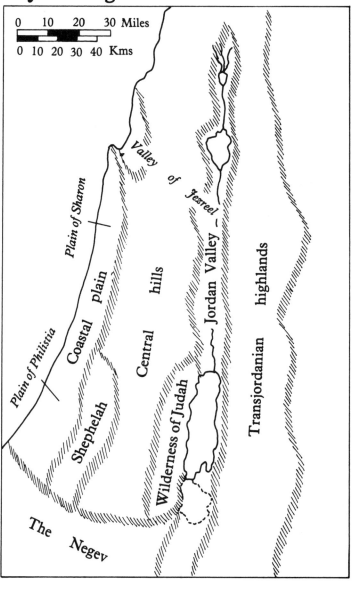

(between the central hills and the Dead Sea). Further south lay the Negev, which will be treated separately.

The coastal plain

The extreme north of Israel's coastal territory encroached onto the plain of Phoenicia. The tribe of Asher was given territory here (Josh 19:24–31), though it failed to take possession of the whole region (Judg 1:31–32). By David's reign, and perhaps through David's conquests, the area was within Israelite control (to judge from 2 Sam 24:7). Just off the coast, on a small island, lay the important Phoenician seaport of Tyre. King Hiram of Tyre had an alliance with David and Solomon (2 Sam 5:11, 1 Kings 5:1–12), and supplied the latter with materials and skilled workmen for building the temple in Jerusalem. He also aided Solomon in his seafaring ventures (1 Kings 9:26–28; 10:11, 22). Links with Tyre were still strong a hundred years later in the time of Ahab, whose notorious wife Jezebel was the daughter of king Ethbaal of Tyre and Sidon (1 Kings 16:31). The wealth and luxury acquired by Tyre as a centre for trade and commerce is depicted in Ezekiel 27.

Opposite Tyre the coastal plain is very narrow, and about nineteen kilometres (twelve miles) to the south it dwindles to almost nothing where the 'Ladder of Tyre', a series of hills running from east to west, approaches the coast. South of this the plain broadens until it is about ten kilometres (six miles) wide opposite the Bay of Haifa. This is a well-watered and fertile region, but with extensive marshes in ancient times. South of the bay the plain is cut off again by Mount Carmel, but south of Carmel it gradually broadens and reaches a width of about nineteen kilometres (twelve miles) where it borders the Shephelah.

In biblical times fishing and agriculture were the basis of settlement along the coast. There were also some ports. Joppa, where Jonah began his flight from God's call (Jon 1:3), was one of the most important. Further inland lay a line of swamps, and east of these a sandstone ridge covered with forests of pine and the deciduous Tabor oak. Beyond this, reaching to the foothills of the central range, was a rich, verdant plain. Indeed, much of the coastal plain was good agricultural land, producing the usual combination of wheat, barley, vines and olives. There was also a major international route running along the coastal plain from

18

Egypt to Syria, the 'way of the sea' (Isa 9:1).

The tribes of Manasseh, Ephraim, Dan and Judah were all allocated territory which reached to the coast (Josh 15:11–12; 16:5–8; 17:9–10; 19:40–46), though none of them enjoyed extensive control over the area because of their failure to dislodge the Canaanites (Judg 1:19, 27, 29, 34). From the twelfth century BC the Philistines were settled in that part of the coastal plain allotted to Judah, and intermittently controlled larger areas until David restricted them once more to the coast (Judg 13–16; 1 Sam 1–17; 31; 2 Sam 5:6–25, etc).

The Shephelah

Lying between the coastal plain and the central hills, the Shephelah extends southwards from the valley of Aijalon. Its name means 'lowlands', but is often not translated in English Bibles. It consists of low, rounded hills divided by broad, fertile valleys, and was a rich agricultural region in biblical times. Sycamores grew extensively there (1 Kings 10:27). These were not the sycamores familiar in Britain and Europe, but a tree bearing a fig-like fruit (Amos 7:14). The region also had vineyards (Judg 14:5) and olive groves. David had an officer 'over the olive and sycamore trees of the Shephelah' (1 Chron 27:28).

The Shephelah fell within the tribal territories of Judah, Benjamin and Dan. It had a number of important cities, notably Lachish, which became Judah's most important city after Jerusalem (see ch 4). Because of its importance agriculturally and as a border area, the Shephelah was often fought over by the Israelites and the Philistines.

The central hill country

Describing this important strip from north to south, we begin with the Galilee region. West of the Sea of Galilee lies the district of Lower Galilee, so called because its highest mountains (nearly 600 metres or 2000 feet) are only half the height of those of Upper Galilee. Most of Upper Galilee, which lies to the north, was historically unimportant because its mountains made settlement and travel difficult. However, on the eastern edge of the Upper Galilee hills, overlooking the Jordan valley, stood Hazor, a major Canaanite city (Josh 11; Judg 4) later rebuilt by Solomon (1 Kings

9: 15). Lower Galilee is endowed with broad valleys connecting the coastal plain with the Sea of Galilee and the Jordan valley.

To the south lies the Esdraelon plain or valley of Jezreel, a great plain running northwest to southeast: from the coastal plain at the Bay of Haifa, connecting at its southeastern end with the Jordan valley. This provided a major route from west to east. The river Kishon flows through it to the coast and there were probably marshes along the river in biblical times. The rest of the plain, however, was valuable agricultural land. Important towns lay around the edges of the valley, such as Jezreel itself, which lay to the southeast near the foothills of the Gilboa mountains. Jezreel became a secondary capital for Israel under Ahab, who had a royal estate there (1 Kings 18: 46; 21: 1–2). It was the scene of horrific bloodshed when Jehu wiped out Ahab's dynasty (2 Kings 9: 30– 10: 11). Across the plain, on the edge of the Carmel range, stood Megiddo, strategically placed at the northern end of a pass which connects the valley of Jezreel with the coast. At the time of the conquest of the land the tribe of Manasseh failed to capture Megiddo and other towns of the region from the Canaanites (Josh 17: 16; Judg 1: 27). These cities were probably incorporated into the kingdom by David, and Megiddo was rebuilt by Solomon (1 Kings 9: 15).

The Carmel range, scene of Elijah's spectacular conflict with the priests of Baal (1 Kings 18), extends from the central hills in a northwesterly direction all the way to the coast. It was well-wooded in biblical times. The passes which cut through it, such as the one guarded by Megiddo, were of immense importance, since they allowed north–south travel and connected the coastal plain with the Jordan valley via the plain of Esdraelon.

Between the Carmel range and the central hills lies the valley of Dothan, and south of this rise the hills of Samaria. This latter region is well-endowed with fertile valleys and small plains and was the location of several important biblical cities. Shechem lay in a valley which has Mount Ebal on its northern side and Mount Gerizim to the south. From these mountains the curses and blessings of the law were to be pronounced (Deut 11: 29; 27: 12–13; Josh 8: 33–34). Joshua built an altar on Mount Ebal (Josh 8: 30– 32), and later renewed Israel's covenant with God at Shechem (Josh 24). Shechem briefly became the capital of the northern tribes when they became independent of Judah (1 Kings 12:25). The city owed its importance to its position, for the valley in which it lay was a major east–west route through the hills, and was joined at Shechem by a road running north–south.

About nine kilometres (six miles) northeast of Shechem lay Tirzah, a city renowned for its beauty (Song of Sol 6:4). For a time it replaced Shechem as Israel's capital (1 Kings 15:21, 33; 16:8, 15, 23), before Omri created a new capital at Samaria (1 Kings 16:24), about fourteen kilometres (nine miles) to the west. Samaria was set on a large hill on the route from Shechem to the coastal plain. It remained Israel's capital until it was destroyed by the Assyrians in 722 BC (see ch 2).

The hill country from the valley of Jezreel as far south as Shechem was allotted to the tribe of Manasseh (which also had territory east of the Jordan). From Shechem southwards to Bethel was 'the hill country of Ephraim' (Judg 7:24, etc). In the southern part of this region the valleys are deep and narrow, providing few major routes and little cultivable land. South of this, however, the hills become lower and gentler. This is the Jerusalem saddle. The natural boundary between these two regions was roughly the border between the tribal territories of Ephraim and Benjamin, and hence between Judah-with-Benjamin and the northern tribes of Israel. On this border lay Bethel, a place associated with Abraham and Jacob (Gen 12:8; 28:10–22; 35:9–15), and an important worship centre for the northern tribes after they split away from Judah (1 Kings 12:26–33; Amos 7:13).

About sixteen kilometres (ten miles) south of Bethel, and thus not far from the northern border of Judah, lay Jerusalem. This was a fairly insignificant town before David's time. It is not situated on a particularly commanding hill, and does not lie far west of the Judean desert. It does, however, lie on a road through the hills which rises from Beersheba in the Negev and passes through Hebron, Bethlehem, Jerusalem, Bethel and on northwards to Shechem (Judg 21:19), where it meets the east–west route mentioned previously. Along the northern edge of the Jerusalem saddle runs the valley of Aijalon, one of the major routes into the hills from the coastal plain, guarded at its western end by Gezer. Other valleys facilitate travel eastwards to the Jordan, the most important being the road from Jerusalem to Jericho. Nevertheless,

Jerusalem's location does not make it an ideal site for a capital city. David probably chose it as such because it had been in Jebusite hands (Judg 1:21; 19:10–12; 2 Sam 5:6–9) and so had not been associated with any particular tribe; its choice would not, therefore, arouse tribal jealousies. If David had not made it his capital, it is unlikely it would ever have become an important city. Other towns of the Jerusalem hills which were significant in the Old Testament period include 'Gibeah of Benjamin' (Saul's capital, 1 Sam 14:16, etc), Gibeon and Mizpah.

South of Bethlehem the hills increase in height once more, reaching about 990 metres (3300 feet). These are the Judean hills, divided by narrow valleys. Here the major town was Hebron, David's capital before the capture of Jerusalem (2 Sam 5:5). Its history stretched back to the days of Abraham (Gen 23 etc) and beyond. The territory of the tribe of Judah is not broken up into numerous contrasting sub-regions like the hills to the north. This probably explains, in fact, why the southern hills were the territory of a single tribe. It also helps to explain why the tribe of Judah became a distinct entity early on (eg 1 Sam 15:4), and why the tribes of Judah and Benjamin (which shared the Jerusalem saddle with Judah) eventually became a separate kingdom.

Although today the hill country is in many places bare and rocky, with limestone outcrops and thin soil cover, in biblical times it was very different. Much of it was heavily forested (Josh 17:15–18; 2 Sam 18:6, etc) with evergreen oak, terebinth, Aleppo pine and cypress. However, there were areas, some of them deliberately cleared of forest, where crops were grown. Wheat grew in the valleys between the hills of Manasseh, and the hill country of Ephraim was ideal for growing olives. Grapes were the staple crop of the Judean hills (Gen 49:11–12; 2 Chron 26:10), though wheat and barley also grew in places (1 Sam 25:18). The area around Bethlehem was a fertile grain-growing district (Ruth 1:22–2:23); indeed, the name of the town means 'House of Bread'.

The Judean desert

East of the Jerusalem saddle and the Judean hills lies an area of very different character. This is the semi-arid Judean desert, where the low rainfall made cultivation and settlement impossible in biblical times. It is not a desert like the Sahara, however; in the winter some parts receive enough rain to be suitable for grazing sheep and goats. The hills descend sharply from over 900 metres (3000 feet) above sea level in the west to 400 metres (1300 feet) *below* sea level at the shore of the Dead Sea. The final drop to this point consists of barren and spectacular cliffs.

The Jordan valley

The Jordan flows through a rift valley which begins in Syria and extends all the way to the Great Lakes region of east Africa. From its sources near the foot of Mount Hermon the river flows through a broad, marshy plain to the Sea of Galilee, nearly 210 metres (690 feet) below sea level. In a mere 104 kilometres (65 miles) as the crow flies it falls to 400 metres (1300 feet) below sea level where it enters the Dead Sea. It is aptly named, for Jordan in Hebrew means 'Descender'.

The river takes a serpentine course through its flood-plain, which is full of luxuriant vegetation, 'the jungle of the Jordan' (Jer 12:5). The water is never deeper than about three metres (ten feet) and not wider than thirty metres (100 feet), and in Old Testament times the river was fordable at a number of places (Josh 2:7; Judg 7:24–8:4; 12:5–6). On the western side of the valley lay two important cities. Jericho, northwest of the Dead Sea, was settled as early as 8000 BC. A fertile oasis made settlement possible, water being produced by an abundant spring, now popularly called Elisha's Spring because of the incident in 2 Kings 2:19–22. Its many date palms gave the city one of its ancient names, the City of Palms (Deut 34:3; Judg 1:16; 3:13). About seventy kilometres (forty-five miles) to the north lay Beth-shan, near one end of an important valley which connected with the valley of Jezreel and so provided a route to the coastal plain.

The eastern side of the Jordan valley had many more important settlements (Succoth, Zarethan, Zaphon, Jabesh-gilead, Pella) than the western side. This is because the east bank has a number of perennial streams, even by the Dead Sea, where Lot was attracted to a region 'like the garden of the Lord' (Gen 13:10).

The shore of the Dead Sea is the lowest point on the earth's surface. For much of its eastern side the sea is bordered by sheer cliffs descending from the mountains of Moab, but between the western shore and the cliffs of the Judean desert is a narrow plain where soft marl terraces have been eroded into weird shapes. On one of these terraces, near the northwestern shore, lies Khirbet Qumran, the ruins of the settlement which produced the Dead Sea Scrolls between about 150 BC and AD 68. At various points freshwater springs give rise to a surprising amount of vegetation, and there were settlements at such places in the biblical period. The best-known spring is En-gedi, where David lived while avoiding Saul (1 Sam 23:29). Its vineyards are mentioned in the Song of Solomon (1:14). The famous salinity of the Dead Sea (called the Salt Sea in Gen 14:3; Num 34:3, etc) is a consequence of the high rate of evaporation.

From the eastern side a peninsula (el-Lisan, 'the Tongue') extends to within three kilometres (two miles) of the western shore. South of this the water is less than six metres (twenty feet) deep (compared with a depth of 400 metres, or 1300 feet, to the north of the Lisan). It is likely that the sea has only encroached here since biblical times, so this southern extension should not be shown on maps which depict the region as it was in the Old Testament period. Sodom, Gomorrah and the other 'cities of the plain' (Gen 14:2) were probably situated in this area.

There is no flow of water south from the Dead Sea. The rift valley continues, however, and meets the eastern arm of the Red Sea (the Gulf of Aqabah) at Elat. Near here Solomon built his port of Ezion-geber (1 Kings 9:26–28).

The Transjordan highlands

East of the Jordan the land rises again to a belt of hills and high plateaux. Further east still, these merge into the great Syrian-Arabian Desert. The Transjordanian hills were an important region of settlement in ancient times, and in the Old Testament period they became the home of various small nation-states: Aram, Ammon, Moab and Edom (in order from north to south).

Numerous streams flowing into the Jordan valley, from the Yarmuk in the north to the Zered in the south, provide abundant water, and the valleys and plateaux are very fertile. Bashan, north of the Yarmuk, was famous for its livestock (Ps 22:12; Ezek 39:18; Amos 4:1, etc). South of the Yarmuk lay Gilead, bisected by the river Jabbok. Here there were rich woodlands (Jer 22:6; 50:19) and fertile grazing land (Song of Sol 4:1; 6:5). Bashan and Gilead were assigned to the tribes of Reuben, Gad and half of Manasseh, but their territories were frequently contested by the Aramaeans, Ammonites and Moabites.

Moab proper lay south of the river Arnon, but the Moabites sometimes extended their territory further north (hence in Num 36:13 and Deut 34:8 'the plains of Moab' refers to the low land across the Jordan from Jericho). One such occasion was in the ninth century BC when Mesha, the king of Moab, successfully rebelled against Israelite rule (2 Kings 3:4–27). As we learn from the Moabite Stone, an inscription in which Mesha celebrates his victory, he captured and rebuilt towns as far north as Heshbon. The region south of the Arnon was dominated by 'the fields of Moab', an extensive, verdant plateau. Crops grew here while areas west of the Jordan suffered famine (Ruth 1:1–2). From the Zered extending towards the Gulf of Aqabah was the territory of Edom. This contained many high, wooded hills, but to the west it bordered on the Arabah, the hot, dry section of the rift valley south of the Dead Sea.

Along the highlands of Transjordan ran an important road known as the King's Highway. This route ran all the way from Damascus to the Gulf of Aqabah and a number of important towns lay along it, including Ramoth-gilead, Heshbon and Dibon. The Israelites tried to travel along this road on their way to Canaan, but were denied passage by the king of Edom and Sihon, king of the Amorites (Num 20:17–18; 21:22–23).

The Negev
Today the biblical term 'Negev' or 'Negeb' (which means 'the dry') is applied to a large, roughly triangular area reaching south from Beersheba to the Gulf of Aqabah. In the Old Testament it is used of a smaller region, the exact limits of which are uncertain. In the view of some scholars, the biblical Negev was a fairly narrow east–west band, extending only about twenty kilometres (twelve miles) north and south of Beersheba. Others think it extended as far south as the oasis of Kadesh-barnea, where the Israelites spent considerable time between the exodus and their final migration to Canaan (Num 13:26; 20:1, etc).

Taking this latter definition of the biblical Negev, it is mostly a high plateau with limestone and sandstone ridges. It is a semi-arid region, but with careful use of the land some cultivation is possible, and there were settlements here in the time of Abraham and again just after the Old Testament period. Beersheba, which lay in an east–west depression marking the northern edge of the Negev, derived great importance from its position. A major route from the coastal plain to the Arabah passed through it, crossing the north–south road from the Hebron hills. This latter joined 'the Way to Shur' (Gen 16:7), another major route which passed along the southern edge of the Negev, leading from the Arabah to Egypt via Kadesh-barnea. It took its name from 'the wilderness of Shur', which lay east of Egypt (Gen 25:18; 1 Sam 27:8). To the south, the Negev shades into 'the wilderness of Paran' in the east–central region of the Sinai peninsula.

In the foregoing pages we have tried to depict the land of Palestine as it was in Old Testament times, rather than describing what a tourist can see in the region today. The appearance of the land has certainly changed since ancient times. Some changes are obvious, of course; the sprawling industrial complexes and skyscraper blocks of modern cities are unlike anything in the ancient world. But there is more to recovering the biblical landscape than mentally removing these recent developments. One notable difference is that the land had far more forests in biblical times than it has today. These have not disappeared because the climate has changed; so far as we can tell, there has been no significant permanent change in the climate since ancient times. The forests have disappeared through human activity over the centuries, beginning in the biblical period itself (Josh 17:15–18). The process was accelerated in recent times, and has had a serious affect on the landscape. Trees prevent soil being washed away by the heavy winter rains, and without this protection the soil has been eroded from many areas, producing the bare hills which can be seen today.

The loss of trees has also meant the disappearance of several animals from the land since Old Testament times. Lions were relatively common (Judg 14:5–6; 2 Sam 23:20; 2 Kings 17:25; Jer 49:19, etc), as was the Syrian brown bear (1 Sam 17:34; 2 Kings 2:24; Amos 5:19), which did not become extinct in Palestine until this century.

Imagining the landscape of the biblical period is only one aspect of entering the world of the Old Testament. We will explore other aspects in the following chapters.

CHAPTER TWO

States and Empires

The relatively small country in which the tribes of Israel settled and came to statehood lay in a position of great importance. Between the Mediterranean to the west and the Syrian-Arabian Desert to the east, it formed a narrow connecting bridge between the great powers of the Ancient Near East. To the south of it lay Egypt, and to the north Syria, Anatolia and northwest Mesopotamia. Israel's territory also lay at the south-western tip of a great arc of cultivable land now known as the Fertile Crescent. This extends northwards to Syria, across northern Mesopotamia and down to the Persian Gulf. The major east-west routes lay within the Fertile Crescent. Abraham's migration clearly followed one such route, though we cannot be sure of the details; leaving Ur in southern Mesopotamia, he moved first to Haran in the northwest (Gen 11:31), and later travelled south into Canaan (12:4-5), even moving briefly into Egypt (12:10). The travels of Abraham introduce us to almost the whole Old Testament world in just a few verses.

The location of her promised land helped shape Israel's history. It is not simply that Israel's near neighbours were great powers. Her location meant that traders and armies moving between (for example) Babylonia and Egypt passed through her territory. It is therefore not surprising that throughout the Old Testament period Israel was involved with the major powers which surrounded her. Because these major powers played such an important part in Israel's history, we should know something about them and their role in the Old Testament world. It is also important to see how Israel's organization as a state compared with that of her neighbours.

As far as possible, the great empires of Egypt, Assyria, Babylon and Persia will be introduced in historical sequence. This way, the history of Israel itself will emerge in outline. Israel's smaller neighbours will then be discussed separately.

The Ancient Near East

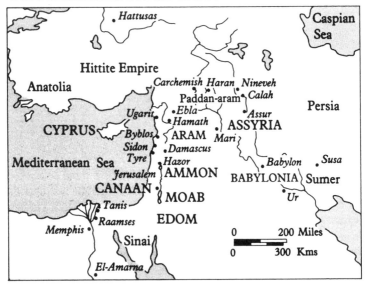

Egypt and its empire

The nearest great power was Egypt, which actually shared a border with Israel in northern Sinai (the Wadi el-Arish, ie the biblical 'Brook of Egypt', Num 34: 5). Egypt's history as a unified kingdom goes back to about 3000 BC. By that early date, Egypt's famous hieroglyphic writing and its characteristic art had both appeared. The land of Egypt was renowned for its fertility, which it owed to the Nile. In times of famine Egypt fared better than the neighbouring lands. Thus it proved attractive to Abraham when Canaan suffered a famine (Gen 12: 10), and the whole family of Jacob later settled there for the same reason (Gen 41–47).

By about 2600 BC Egypt had begun its first period of great prosperity and achievement, known as the Old Kingdom (2575–2134 BC). It was during this period that the three famous pyramids were built at Giza. After a brief time of political weakness, Egypt achieved greatness again during the Middle Kingdom (2040–1650 BC). Abraham's visit to Egypt should probably be placed early in this period. There was fairly close contact between Egypt and Canaan throughout the Middle Kingdom; Egyptian objects found in excavations in Palestine are probably evidence for trade with Egypt, and there is evidence from Egypt itself that from around 1850 BC people from Canaan were moving into the north-eastern parts of the Nile Delta and settling there. The Hebrews were almost certainly among these settlers, as the Middle Kingdom is the most likely period for Joseph's rise to high office (Gen 39–45) and the migration of the rest of Jacob's family into Egypt (Gen 46–47). By the end of the period, the Egyptians had made the Hebrews their slaves (Exod 1: 8–14).

From about 1650–1550 BC, Egypt was under the rule of foreigners whom the Egyptians called the Hyksos. Shortly after 1550 BC, the Hyksos were defeated and driven out of Egypt, and Egypt once again began a magnificent recovery. This was the period of the New Kingdom (1550–1070 BC), during which the Hebrew tribes were led out of slavery by Moses. The exact date of the exodus is debated. A chronological note given by the Bible itself (1 Kings 6: 1) suggests a date around 1450 BC, in which case the pharaoh of the exodus would have been Thutmose III (1490–1436 BC). On the other hand, the Bible also says the enslaved Hebrews built for the pharaoh a city called Raamses (Exod 1:11), and this calls to mind the great building projects of Ramesses II (1290–1224 BC), who did indeed create a city named after himself (Pi-Ramesse, which means 'Domain of Ramesses') in the eastern Nile Delta. On the basis of this latter piece of evidence, some scholars date the exodus to about 1260 BC. Both Thutmose III and Ramesses II were strong pharaohs who would fit well the Bible's picture of the pharaoh of the exodus (Exodus 5–14).

During the New Kingdom, the relationship between Egypt and Canaan changed. Canaan became part of an extensive Egyptian empire created by Thutmose III. This great warrior-pharaoh led his armies several times into Palestine, and often through Palestine into Syria to the north. Rulers of Palestine's cities became Egypt's vassals, and Egyptian governors were placed over them. Egyptian troops were installed in Gaza, Joppa, Megiddo, Beth-shan, Ashdod and half a dozen other towns. The garrisons consisted of infantry and chariots, and at Joppa there was an Egyptian chariot workshop. Towns in fertile areas had to contribute to the rations of the Egyptian troops, as well as sending tribute to Egypt. It is unlikely that Palestine itself provided Egypt with great wealth, but it was important for Egypt to control it because major trade-routes ran through it, and because Palestine was Egypt's corridor to Syria, where her armies could be needed at any time to guard the northern limits of her empire.

By about 1400 BC Egypt was the richest and most powerful nation in the civilized world. Her empire was at its height, stretching from Nubia in the south to Ugarit (on the coast of Syria) in the north. The empire's northern extent was limited by two powerful neighbours: the Hittite empire, centred in Anatolia, and the kingdom of Mitanni in northern Mesopotamia. Egypt had also extended its influence across the waves of the Mediterranean. Thutmose III had built a navy, and an inscription dating from about 1400 BC contains a list of Greek and Cretan place-names, showing the extent of Egypt's overseas contacts by that time.

Egypt's control over her empire may have slackened around 1350 BC, but only temporarily. In the next century Ramesses II campaigned vigorously, and several times led his armies through Palestine to fight against the Hittites in Syria. These clashes ended with a peace treaty and Ramesses' marriage to a Hittite princess.

The city-states of Canaan

In all, Egypt kept its empire for some three hundred years, from about 1450 to about 1150 BC. During this time, Canaan itself consisted of several small city-states; that is, each city and its surrounding territory comprised a separate mini-state with its own ruler. This is why, in the Bible's account of Israel's conquest of Canaan under Joshua, we are told of the defeat of numerous 'kings' (Josh 5–12). This is the Bible's way of referring to the rulers of the individual city-states.

At the centre of each city-state was the city itself. In some periods (eg that which archaeologists call the Middle Bronze Age, about 2000–1500 BC) these were surrounded by large fortifications and must have looked something like huge medieval castles. But during the time when Palestine was part of the Egyptian empire, only a few cities had such walls. This was perhaps because the Egyptian administrators wanted to limit their strength to prevent them rebelling against the pharaoh's control. Each city was a centre for administration, industry and trade. The territory controlled by each city would typically contain a number of small villages, agricultural land and land for grazing flocks. Leaving aside the Egyptian administrators, each city would be under the direct control of its ruler ('king') and his personnel. The craftsmen, traders, and villagers who worked the fields all worked in effect for the king. Canaanite society also contained people who were not part of the city-state system at all – nomadic groups who from time to time settled temporarily near the cities (as we find Abraham, Isaac and Jacob doing in the Old Testament, eg Gen 20, 26, 33: 18).

We will be looking in more detail at city life in the Old Testament period in chapter 4. For now we should simply notice how uncertain life must have been. The rulers of the city-states did not like being subject to overlords such as the Egyptians, and seized any opportunity to rebel which presented itself. This would provoke an Egyptian campaign to remove the rebellious vassal, who would either be killed or taken captive to Egypt, along with his family. In such a campaign, the whole city might suffer a siege (see ch 6 on siege warfare). In addition to unstable relations with the ruling power, there was sometimes war between neighbouring city-states, usually over the control of territory. Sometimes the great empires themselves were in conflict, as when Egypt fought the Hittites in the thirteenth century BC, and the city-states would be caught in the middle, finding themselves fought over. The world of the city-states was therefore a world of shifting alliances in which ordinary people could be caught up unexpectedly in clashes between states and empires.

The arrival of Israel in Canaan

The period of Egyptian control of Canaan (about 1450–1150 BC) is also the period during which the Israelites must have entered the land under Joshua. The exact date of their arrival is debated, and naturally depends on which of the two possible dates we prefer for the exodus (see above). With the earlier date for the exodus, the Israelites would have entered Canaan just before 1400 BC. With the later date, they would have arrived shortly before 1200 BC.

Whatever its date, their arrival, and their conquest of certain city-states, must have brought change and upheaval to some areas, though the impact was perhaps not so great as we might at first imagine from reading Joshua 1–12. A careful reading of the later chapters of the book of Joshua (chs 13–21), and the first chapter of the book of Judges, shows that the Israelite conquest was by no means complete. In particular, the main Canaanite cities in the plains and along the coast were not conquered. The trade routes and the coastal road to Syria were therefore not threatened, and the Egyptian administration probably lost little sleep over the influx of new settlers. An important set of documents from around 1350 BC, known as the Amarna Letters, shows us something of the Egyptian attitude to Palestine's internal problems. These are letters from the rulers of the Palestinian city-states to the pharaoh Akhenaten, and they show us a land torn by intrigue and conflict between city-states, often involving *ḥabiru*, a term for people who were not part of the city-state system. It seems from this correspondence that Egyptian interference was minimal. Egypt was only concerned to stop internal squabbles if her own interests were threatened. This was probably true of the whole period for which Egypt controlled Palestine. As for the Hebrew settlers themselves, some perhaps retained the nomadic ways of their wilderness wanderings for a while; others, however, were soon absorbed into the city-state system (see Judg 1:29–33).

At the end of the period which archaeologists call the Late Bronze Age (about 1500–1200 BC), the political picture of the Ancient Near East changed dramatically. Within a fairly short time, the great power blocs vanished. Shortly after 1200 BC the Hittite empire collapsed as a result of attacks from the west, and by 1150 BC Egypt had become weak and her empire slipped from her grasp. The reasons for these changes are still not properly understood by archaeologists and ancient historians. Perhaps a slight change of climate caused famines, and so sparked off migrations and invasions which weakened the great empires. Certainly, some peoples were on the move around 1200 BC. Ramesses III (1194–1163 BC) defended Egypt against attacks by 'Peoples of the Sea' and other groups. These included the Philistines, who settled in the southern part of Palestine's coastal plain around that time.

For a while Assyria seemed poised to move into the vacuum left by the Egyptian and Hittite empires. Assyria lay south of the old territory of the kingdom of Mitanni, and had begun to gain power when Mitanni declined in the fourteenth century BC. Tiglath-pileser I of Assyria (1115–1077 BC) brought his armies as far west as the Mediterranean coast and took tribute from Byblos, Sidon and Arvad. But from about 1100 to 940 BC the attacks of desert tribes kept the Assyrian armies too busy to make further campaigns to the west. This meant that by 1050 BC there was no major power in control of Palestine and Syria. By then the city-state system had also more or less collapsed, the cities of the Late Bronze Age being replaced from about 1200 BC by smaller, more widely-scattered settlements. Many of these new settlements were doubtless the work of the Israelites. The scene was therefore set for the creation of a new state in the region, the Hebrew monarchy of Saul, David and Solomon.

Israel's first kings

It is worth pausing to ask why Israel became a monarchy when it did. It appears that in the eleventh century BC the Israelites were threatened simultaneously by the Philistines from the west (1 Sam

9: 16) and the Ammonites from the east (11: 1; 12: 12), and initially wanted a king in the form of a military leader ('that our king may govern us and go out before us and fight our battles', 1 Sam 8: 20). Previously, tribal leaders (the 'judges') had led individual tribes or small confederations of tribes in battle (as we see from the book of Judges). While the conflicts were relatively localized, affecting only one or a few of the tribes, this kind of spontaneous, charismatic leadership was successful. However, the imperialism of the Philistines meant that Israel had to fight in a concerted way to retain its land.

It seems from 1 Samuel 8: 5, 19–20 that Israel was deliberately imitating other nations in adopting kingship. But which nations? Certainly not the Canaanites who, as we have seen, had kings ruling separate city-states. (Though earlier Abimelech had been made king of the city of Shechem after the Canaanite pattern; Judg 9.) Nor was Israel imitating the Philistines, who were organized into a league of five city-states (Josh 13: 3). The nations whose pattern Israel followed were the nation-states of Transjordan, that is, Edom, Moab and Ammon, all of which had kings before Israel (see Gen 36: 31; Num 20: 14; 22: 4; 1 Sam 12: 12).

However, it would be wrong to think that Israel became a fully-developed nation-state overnight. As noted already, the first king, Saul (about 1045–1011/1010 BC), seems to have been little more than a military leader. Conscription may have been introduced to create an army, but the Bible contains no hints that a centralized administration was developed. It would probably be technically correct to describe Israel under Saul as a chiefdom, a halfway stage between a tribal society and a state. The change to full statehood came with David and Solomon.

David (1011/1010–971/970 BC) developed Jerusalem as a new capital, and created a complex bureaucracy around him. As well as a commander of the army (2 Sam 8: 16; 19: 13), thirty or so crack troops ('mighty men', 2 Sam 23: 8ff) and a commander of foreign mercenaries (2 Sam 8: 18), David had numerous treasurers, officers and officials (2 Sam 8: 16–17; 1 Chron 26: 26). Once David's conquests had created a mini-empire, a centralized bureaucracy would have been essential to administer it properly.

The empire created by David included the neighbouring states to the north and east. In the absence of any major power to the

The Kingdom of Saul

The Empire of David and Solomon

Approximate limits of the Kingdom of Saul

Territory under vassal treaty

Boundary of empire at its greatest extent

Territory conquered by David

north, David was able to conquer the small states of Syria (2 Sam 8:3–12; 10:6–19), apparently extending Israelite control as far as the Euphrates (see the extent of Solomon's empire in 2 Chron 9:26). He also conquered Edom, Moab and Ammon to the east of the Jordan (2 Sam 8:2, 13–14; 12:26–31).

Egypt became an ally of the newly-merged state. Solomon (971/970–931/930 BC) married a daughter of the pharaoh (1 Kings 9:16; also 7:8; 11:1), and there were important trade links between the two countries during his reign (10:28–29). After Solomon's death, however, the alliance broke down; the pharaoh Shishak (Shoshenq I, 945–924 BC) invaded Palestine and denuded Jerusalem of its treasures (1 Kings 14:25–26). But this was not a resurgence of Egypt's own days of empire. In the following decades the major threats to Israel and Judah came from the north, not from the south, as we will see below.

Solomon continued David's work of transforming the state, setting up officers over twelve new administrative districts. Their chief role seems to have been to administer a taxation system which supplied food for the palace households (1 Kings 4:7–19) and provisions for the royal stables (4:28). To judge from 1 Kings 4:22–28 the requirements of the palace must have been an enormous burden on the population. The twelve administrative districts had nothing to do with the traditional tribal territories (except that Judah kept its identity as a separate district in the south), and their creation must have completely transformed Israelite society. Along with the heavy taxation and the system of conscripted labour, this must have contributed to the tension which led the northern tribes to break away from Judah after Solomon's death (1 Kings 12).

Although kingship in Israel was, as we have seen, patterned on that of existing nation-states, it was in some respects distinctive, because of Israel's distinctive religious beliefs. The king could not be thought of as identical with his god, as in Egypt, as this would have been abhorrent to Israelite faith; nor was he the god's representative, as in Assyria. He was, however, divinely appointed; he was God's king, that is, crowned and anointed by God (eg Ps 89:18–20), and also God's 'servant' (Pss 78:70; 89:3, 20). This latter title was the one borne in the Ancient Near East by a vassal king. It signifies that for Israel it was God who was the supreme ruler.

The divided kingdom and Assyria

The division of the monarchy at Solomon's death meant a weakening of Israel's position in a number of ways. There were now two distinct states, Israel in the north and Judah in the south, each with its own king. As might be expected, the empire created by David's conquests fell apart, and Israel and Judah, at war with each other, were vulnerable to attack from outside.

Even before Solomon's death, a state within Israel's small empire had broken free and become an enemy, namely the state of Aram ('Syria' in some English Bibles) ruled from Damascus by Rezon (1 Kings 11:23–25). After the division of the kingdom, Aram increased in power and extent, and during the ninth century BC, in the reign of Ben-Hadad I, began to threaten Israel. The wars between Aram and Israel's king Ahab (874/73–858 BC) form the background to 1 Kings 20, 22, and later battles provide the setting for the stories of Elisha (2 Kings 2–13). Under Hazael and his son Ben-Hadad II, Israel was reduced to very desperate straits indeed (2 Kings 13: 3–7), and even Judah was threatened (2 Kings 12: 17–18). But around 800 BC Aram was weakened by the advance into the west of the armies of Assyria, and under Jeroboam II (793/2–753 BC) Israel regained its lost territory and embarked on a new era of political strength (2 Kings 14: 25–28).

Israel itself had clashed with Assyria some while earlier, though the Old Testament does not mention the event. We learn of it from the inscriptions of the Assyrian king Shalmaneser III (858–824 BC). Shalmaneser had captured the city of Carchemish, in Syria, in 857 BC, and in response to that a coalition of ten western kings opposed him at Qarqar in 853 BC. Shalmaneser records that among the forces ranged against him were 2000 chariots and 10,000 men supplied by 'Ahab the Israelite'. The battle was apparently indecisive, but by 841 BC the coalition had evidently collapsed. Shalmaneser records that in that year he received tribute from Tyre, Sidon, and from Jehu, king of Israel. The payment of tribute to Assyria by Jehu in the first year of his reign (841–814/13 BC) is another event known to us only from the Assyrian texts. On this occasion, the Assyrian threat did not last. By Shalmaneser III's death in 824 BC, his empire had been weakened by rebellion and all its western holdings were lost. Apart from campaigns by Adad-nirari III around 800 BC, in one of which Damascus was crushed, Assyrian interference in the west was not resumed until 745 BC, when the vigorous king Tiglath-pileser III (745–727 BC) embarked on a new phase of deliberate imperialism. This had very serious consequences for both Israel and Judah. The terror inspired by the Assyrian army in this period is vividly captured in Isaiah 5: 26–30:

> Their arrows are sharp,
> all their bows bent,
> their horses' hoofs seem like flint,
> and their wheels like the whirlwind.
> Their roaring is like a lion,
> like young lions they roar;
> they growl and seize their prey,
> they carry it off and none can rescue (28–29).

From Tiglath-pileser III onwards, Assyria had a threefold system of dealing with subject states. Some states became Assyrian satellites by submitting voluntarily. As a sign of their submission to Assyrian overlordship, gifts and annual tribute were sent; naturally, such states also had to support Assyria in military ventures. Assyrian interference was usually minimal in these circumstances. However, in the case of a kingdom, city or people which refused to submit voluntarily, or of a satellite which rebelled against Assyrian authority, overlordship was imposed by conquest, and the state became a vassal. A native king would still be allowed to rule, provided he remained loyal to Assyria, but Assyrian officials played a larger part in the life of a vassal state, ensuring that Assyria's interests were being served. A third kind of status was reserved for a vassal state which tried to rebel. (Rebellion was usually signalled by withholding the annual tribute.) Such rebel states were turned into provinces. This often involved the destruction of major cities to punish the rebellion, the deportation of the cream of the population, and replacing the native ruler with an Assyrian military governor. Foreign populations from other parts of the Assyrian empire would be brought in to resettle the new province.

All three types of subjugation are found in the histories of Israel and Judah. Israel actually experienced all three in succession. In 738 BC (the year is known from Assyrian records of the event), Menahem submitted voluntarily to Tiglath-pileser III (2 Kings 15:19–20, where he is called Pul). A few years later, under Pekah, Israel joined with Damascus and other states in an anti-Assyrian rebellion. Tiglath-pileser III moved to crush this in 734–732 BC, and the northern part of Israel was converted into a province, while the rest became a vassal state under Hoshea (2 Kings 15:29–30). We know from the Assyrian records that Hoshea, who assassinated Pekah, was confirmed on the throne in Samaria by Tiglath-pileser III in 732 BC. Later, however, Hoshea withheld tribute from Tiglath-pileser's successor Shalmaneser V (726–722 BC), and as a consequence Samaria was besieged. After three years it fell and was destroyed in 722/21 BC. This was the end of Israel, the northern kingdom, which was reorganized as an Assyrian province (2 Kings 17:3–6, 24). The process was completed by Shalmaneser's successor Sargon II (721–705 BC), who has left inscriptions dealing with Samaria's destruction and its redevelopment as an Assyrian administrative centre.

Judah almost suffered the same fate. When threatened by Pekah of Israel and his ally Rezin of Damascus, Ahaz (744/43–716/15 BC) voluntarily submitted to Tiglath-pileser III in return for Assyria's aid. Thus in 734 BC Judah became an Assyrian satellite. Later, under Hezekiah (716/15–687/86 BC, co-regent with Ahaz from about 727), Judah was involved in an anti-Assyrian rebellion, and in 701 BC Jerusalem was threatened by the armies of Sennacherib (704–681 BC). The city was miraculously delivered (2 Kings 18–19), but we learn from Assyrian texts that Judah was an Assyrian vassal for much of the next century.

Judah's freedom came with the weakening of Assyria around 630 BC. At about that date, overstretched by its cumbersome empire, Assyria went into a rapid decline. In 612 BC, with the fall of Nineveh to the Babylonians and Medes, its empire was finished. However, Judah's freedom was short-lived and far from peaceful. In 609 BC, an Egyptian army led by pharaoh Neco II marched north through Palestine to give the last remnant of Assyria aid against Babylon. Judah's king Josiah (640/39–609 BC) tried to stop him, but died in the attempt (2 Kings 23:29–30). However, his intervention may not have been in vain, for Neco's efforts to shore up Assyrian power failed, perhaps because Josiah delayed his advance. On the other hand, Judah was now a vassal-state of Egypt (2 Kings 23:31–35).

The Neo-Babylonian empire and Judah's exile

There was to be no return to the days of an Egyptian empire in Syria and Palestine. In 605 BC Nebuchadnezzar, king of Babylon (605–562 BC), defeated Egyptian forces as Carchemish, and the whole of Syria-Palestine passed into his control (2 Kings 24:7; Jer 46:2). Judah thus exchanged Egyptian for Babylonian vassaldom (2 Kings 24:1), becoming part of Nebuchadnezzar's Neo-Babylonian empire.

Following this, events tragically followed the pattern in Israel just over a century before. Around 601 BC Jehoiakim of Judah rebelled, and in 598 BC Nebuchadnezzar besieged Jerusalem, an event recorded in the Babylonian Chronicle as well as in the Old Testament (2 Kings 24: 8–17). The city was not destroyed, but part of the population was deported and the king replaced with one expected to be more loyal. After a few more years, however, this king, Zedekiah, also rebelled. On this occasion the outcome was the destruction of Jerusalem by Nebuchadnezzar's armies, followed by further deportations (2 Kings 25: 1–22). Thus in 587 BC Judah's exile in Babylon began.

We should not imagine the land a deserted waste during this period. People were left to farm it on behalf of the Babylonian administration (2 Kings 25: 12). But educated and skilled people were deported, and with Jerusalem and its Temple in ruins the future looked very bleak. However, there was a significant difference between the treatment of deportees by Assyria and Babylon. The Assyrians seem to have dispersed deported populations, so that all trace of national identity was lost. This is what happened to the northern tribes after Samaria fell in 722 BC. The people of Judah experienced a different kind of exile, evidently living in settlements in which national identity was preserved (Ezek 1: 1; 3: 15; 20: 1). Thus for Judah there was hope for the future, though it may not have seemed like it at the time.

Many of the Jews in Babylon were probably given land to farm. As tenants of the king, however, they would have been required to provide labour for building projects, pay taxes, and do military service. On the other hand, not all Jews in Babylon served their captors in menial roles. The book of Daniel shows that some became high-ranking civil servants in the Babylonian administration. Daniel himself became 'ruler over the whole province of Babylon, and chief prefect over all the wise men of Babylon'; his three friends were also appointed to high office (Dan 2: 48–49).

The Persian empire and Judah's return

In 539 BC another nation succeeded Babylon as the major power of the east. In that year Babylon fell to Cyrus, king of Persia, and under Cyrus's rule the Jews in Babylon were allowed to return to Judah and rebuild their city and Temple (Ezra 1: 1–11).

However, by no means all exiled Jews chose to return to Judah.

Hence in the following century we find Jews living in Susa, the Persian capital (Neh 1: 1; Est 2: 5ff) and, indeed, there were Jewish communities throughout the vast Persian empire (Est 8: 9; 9: 30). It is likely that many Jews had come to enjoy relative prosperity during the exile and had little incentive to leave the new lives they had created for themselves.

The Old Testament gives us glimpses of the complex administrative system by which this empire was governed. Esther 8: 9 speaks of 127 provinces stretching from India to Ethiopia, ruled by satraps, governors and princes. A satrap was the ruler of a satrapy. Probably under Darius I (522–486 BC) the empire was divided into twenty satrapies, each consisting of several smaller provinces. Judah was a province within the satrapy 'Beyond the River' (Euphrates; Neh 2: 9; 3: 7), which consisted of all Syria-Palestine. The various official letters quoted in the books of Ezra and Nehemiah reflect the central administration's concern for relatively minor matters in distant parts of the empire. Ezra and Nehemiah both carried out their missions with the full support of the administration, and Nehemiah was appointed governor of Judah in 445 BC.

When the Persian empire fell to Alexander the Great in 333 BC, this still did not mean independence for Judah, for it remained a province of the Greek empire. Only in 128 BC was independence regained, under the Hasmonean priest-kings, and then only briefly. In 63 BC Judah, now Judea, became part of the Roman empire. This was still the situation when the New Testament period began.

Israel's nearest neighbours

We will now add a little more detail to our sketch of the political world of the Old Testament, by introducing those small states which were Israel's nearest neighbours. These have already been mentioned in passing, but additional information will be provided here.

West: the Philistines

To the west, along the coastal plain, were the Philistines, actually occupying territory allotted to Israel (Num 34:6; Josh 13:2). Like the Israelites themselves, the Philistines were foreigners to the land of Canaan. The prophet Amos says they came from Caphtor (Amos 9:7), which many scholars believe to be Crete, though some prefer Cyprus. The Old Testament speaks of Philistines living in the southern part of the coastal plain at an early period (Gen 26), but texts outside the Bible do not speak of them until the twelfth century BC (ie in the time of the judges). Then we read of them attacking Egypt along with other groups (collectively known as 'Peoples of the Sea') in the reign of Ramesses III (1194–1163 BC). Ramesses successfully repulsed the invaders, and at roughly that time their distinctive type of pottery appears along Palestine's coastal plain south of Mt Carmel. If this was the first influx of Philistines into Canaan, then the references to their presence in earlier periods must be anachronistic. However, it may be that previous settlements of Philistines, or related groups, had occurred on a smaller scale.

The five major Philistine cities were Gaza, Ashdod, Ashkelon, Gath and Ekron (Josh 13:3, etc), each under a *seren*, which the RSV translates as 'ruler' or 'lord'. These cities were organized into a league, hence the Old Testament speaks of 'the five lords of the Philistines' (Judg 3:3).

It was certainly after the influx in the twelfth century BC that the Philistines began to contest Israel's possession of the land (Judg 13–16; 1 Sam 4ff). David eventually broke their power and limited them to the coastal plain (2 Sam 5:17–25). There were, however, continuing conflicts over the Shephelah (1 Kings 15:27; 2 Chron 21:16–17; 26:6), and a particularly serious Philistine incursion took place in the reign of Ahaz (744/43–716/15 BC). Several towns in the Shephelah lost to the Philistines (2 Chron 28:18), but Judah appears to have regained them in the reign of Hezekiah (2 Kings 18:8). The last Old Testament reference to the Philistines comes from Zechariah in the post-exilic period (Zech 9:5–7).

The religion of the Philistines does not betray their foreign origins, and they seem to have become thoroughly Canaanite in this respect. They worshipped Ashtaroth, Baal-zebub and Dagon (Judg 16:23; 1 Sam 5:1–5; 31:10; 2 Kings 1:1–6), all of which were revered widely in the Ancient Near East.

Israel's nearest neighbours

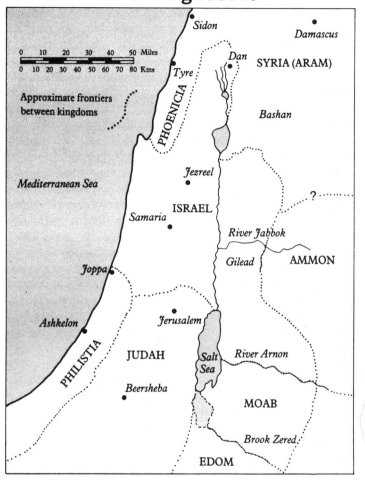

Sidon

Damascus

0 10 20 30 40 50 Miles

0 10 20 30 40 50 60 70 80 Kms

Dan

SYRIA (ARAM)

Tyre

PHOENICIA

Approximate frontiers
between kingdoms

Bashan

Mediterranean Sea

Jezreel

ISRAEL

?

Samaria

River Jabbok

Gilead

AMMON

Joppa

Ashkelon

Jerusalem

PHILISTIA

JUDAH

Salt
Sea

River Arnon

Beersheba

MOAB

Brook Zered

EDOM

North: Phoenicians

In the north, Israel shared the coastal plain with the Phoenicians. The Phoenicians were effectively the remnant of the original Canaanite population, reduced to this northern coastal territory by the invasions of the Israelites and Philistines in the south and by Aramean pressure in the north. They became an adventurous seafaring people, with colonies in Sardinia, Cyprus, Tunisia, Sicily and north Africa (Carthage). The close links which David and Solomon had with Tyre, the chief Phoenician port of their day, have already been outlined in chapter 1. Tyre and Sidon, another major city, are frequently mentioned by the prophets (eg Isa 23; Jer 47:4; Ezek 27–28; Zech 9:2–4), and we get vivid glimpses of the wealth and luxury which maritime trade brought to the Phoenician ports (see especially Ezek 27:1–25).

East: Edom, Moab, Amorites, Ammonites

To the east of the Jordan lay the territories of Edom, Moab, the Amorites and Ammonites. These were all states with their own kings by the time Israel began her migration towards Canaan after forty years in the wilderness. Indeed, their kings opposed Israel's passage through their territories (Num 20–24). It has often been stated that these events could not have occurred before the thirteenth century BC, because for hundreds of years before that date there were no settled populations in Transjordan. However, recent archaeological surveys and excavations have shown this conclusion to be wrong, based as it was on insufficient evidence. Transjordan was never without a settled population, though between the twentieth and thirteenth centuries BC the population may have been somewhat less than at other times. This means we simply do not know how early these kingdoms emerged.

The southernmost of these states was Edom. At the time of Israel's journey towards Canaan, the king of Edom seems to have ruled a large area, from Kadesh-barnea in the west to somewhere beyond the King's Highway in the east (Num 20:16–17), and probably reaching as far south as the Gulf of Aqabah. Thus he was able to deny Israel access to the King's Highway (Num 20:20–21). In later periods Edom seems to have been confined to territory east of the Arabah. Saul campaigned against Edom (1 Sam 14:47), and David incorporated it into his empire (2 Sam 8:12, 14). However,

Edom later rebelled against Judah (2 Kings 8:20–22) and is frequently spoken of by the prophets as one of Judah's bitterest enemies (Jer 49:7–22; Obad 1–14, etc). When Jerusalem fell to the Babylonians in 587 BC, Edomites moved into the area south of Hebron, and this region therefore became known as Idumea.

The boundary between Edom and Moab was the Wadi Zered (Num 21:11–12), and that between Moab and Ammon was the River Arnon (Num 21:13). As we saw in chapter 1, however, there were times when Moab controlled territory further north than this. It seems that when Moses led Israel through Transjordan, Moab had recently lost land north of the Arnon to Sihon, king of the Amorites, who ruled from Heshbon (Num 21:26–30). David subjugated Moab (2 Sam 8:2), but it must have subsequently rebelled, perhaps when the kingdom divided. We know this because the Moabite Stone, an inscription erected in Dibon (the Moabite capital) by king Mesha, refers to Moab's (re)conquest by Omri, father of Ahab. This must have occurred around 880 BC. The Old Testament's brief record of Omri's reign does not mention it, though we do read of Mesha's successful rebellion against Israel in 2 Kings 3:4–27. It is this rebellion which the Moabite Stone celebrates, as we mentioned in chapter 1.

North of the Arnon as far north as the Jabbok was traditionally the territory of the Ammonites (Deut 2:18–21), but at the time of Moses the Amorites under Sihon appear to have pushed the Ammonites eastwards beyond the Jabbok's southern arm (Num 21:24). Israel defeated Sihon in battle (Num 21:23–25) and took his territory, but did not encroach on that of the Ammonites (Deut 2:19). In later centuries the Ammonites became the dominant power in that area and made war on the Israelites (Judg 11:4–33). David defeated them and incorporated Ammon into his empire (2 Sam 12:26–31), but we find Ammonites raiding Judah along with Moabites and Edomites in the reign of Jehoshaphat (2 Chron 20:1–30), perhaps around 850 BC. In the following century Judah was once again receiving tribute from the Ammonites (2 Chron 26:8; 27:5), but they reappear as Judah's enemies (along with the Moabites) around the time of Jerusalem's fall to the Babylonians (2 Kings 24:2; Jer 40:14).

The Old Testament acknowledges racial links between Israel and the Edomites, Moabites and Ammonites. The Edomites are depicted as the descendants of Esau, Jacob's brother (Gen 36: 1), while the Moabites and Ammonites are said to be descended from the sons of Lot (Gen 19: 37–38).

Bashan and Aram

In the time of Moses the region of Bashan, east of the Sea of Galilee, was under a king called Og. The Israelites defeated him and slaughtered his people, taking possession of their territory (Num 21: 33–35). There was no resurgence of this kingdom in later centuries. Instead, it was Israel's more northerly neighbour, the Aramean state of Damascus, which posed a grave threat to Israel in this area (2 Kings 10: 32–33). As we saw earlier, Israel's losses to the Arameans were regained by Jeroboam II (2 Kings 14: 25, 28). However, the northern part of Transjordan was subsequently taken from Israel by Tiglath-pileser III (2 Kings 15: 29) and reorganized as Assyrian provinces.

We have now completed our brief survey of Israel's setting and her involvement with the states and empires around her. We see how her neighbours constantly impinged upon her, helping to shape her history. The Bible reminds us, however, that it was ultimately God who shaped Israel's history; even great empires are his tools and servants (Isa 10: 5–6; 45: 1–13; Jer 27: 6–7).

CHAPTER THREE

Pastoral Nomads and Village Farmers

In this chapter and the next we will look at ways people lived in the Old Testament world, examining three different lifestyles in turn. In this chapter we will examine the lifestyles of pastoral nomads and village farmers, and in the following chapter we will turn our attention to life in the cities. The topics are presented this way for the sake of convenience, and their order does *not* mean that these three lifestyles developed one after the other. As we shall see, all three ways of living were often contemporary and related to each other. For reasons of space, we will concentrate almost entirely on how the Israelites lived *in Palestine*.

Living in tents

Israel's ancestors, the patriarchs Abraham, Isaac and Jacob, lived in tents and led a semi-nomadic lifestyle, frequently relocating their settlements. After the exodus from Egypt we find the whole nation leading a similar existence in the wilderness south of Canaan. Even after their entry into the promised land the Israelites continued living in tents for a while (Josh 3:14; 7:21–24; 22:4–8). The Old Testament knows, however, that other people were living in permanent villages and cities while the nation's ancestors were tent-dwellers, and that city life had its origins in the very remote past (Gen 4:17). Archaeology has revealed cities as much as 10,000 years old, one of the oldest being at Jericho. By 7000 BC this walled town covered ten acres and had an estimated 2000 inhabitants.

The world of Abraham, Isaac and Jacob therefore contained many cities, some of them already ancient, and the lifestyle of the patriarchs involved them in frequent contacts with city life. Indeed, since Abraham's family came from 'Ur of the Chaldees' (Gen 11:28, 31), one of the major cities of southern Mesopotamia, they may have been city-dwellers themselves, or they may have lived in a village under the jurisdiction of the great city. After their migration from Ur to Haran, in northwest Mesopotamia, part of the family resumed a settled existence once again (Gen 11:31–32). We find that branch of the family still living near Haran in the lifetimes of Isaac and Jacob (Gen 24:10; 28:2, 10; 29:4, etc). The town where they lived is not named, but it would seem to have been an agricultural village of the sort described later in this chapter; the family was engaged in rearing sheep (29:9–10; 30:29–43), and they kept provender for animals in or next to their houses (24:25–32).

The lifestyle of the patriarchs
The group which moved on with Abraham into Canaan lived as pastoral nomads. Although the narrative often says that Abraham, Isaac or Jacob 'pitched his tent' in such-and-such a place (eg Gen 12:8; 26:25; 33:19), we must not imagine that one tent housed the whole group. The Old Testament itself speaks in places of several separate tents (eg 31:33). As well as the patriarchs' large families, there were also herdsmen and male and female servants attached to the household (12:16; 13:7–8; 24:35; 32:13–15). When Lot's family needed rescuing from an alliance of invading kings, Abraham was able to gather 318 fighting men from among his household (14:14). This suggests a total of several hundred people for the whole group. In keeping with this, we read that Abimelech, king of the city of Gerar, felt threatened by Isaac's household (26:14–16). The tents of the patriarchs' families and servants must have comprised a very extensive encampment. The tents themselves

A Bedouin tent. The front flap is removed during the day for ventilation, to let in light and provide easy access.

were probably similar to those used by Bedouin families today: rectangular in shape, the fabric consisting of animal skin or goats' hair, supported by poles and held firm by cords and stakes (see Isa 54: 2). The wives of the patriarchs evidently had their own tents (Gen 24: 67, NIV; 31: 33), probably next to, and perhaps connected with, those of their husbands.

The patriarchal practice of having more than one wife was in keeping with customs which were widespread at that time. We learn from a variety of ancient texts that it was customary for a man to have a second wife if his first wife could not provide him with children. In some texts it is the barren wife's responsibility to provide the second wife for her husband, and this is what happened in the cases of Abraham and Sarah (Gen 16: 1–2) and Jacob and Rachel (30: 1–3). Leah took similar action when she found she could have no more children (30: 9).

The movements of the patriarchs were not usually over great distances. The original migrations from Ur to Haran and from there to Canaan were exceptional, as was Jacob's journey to Paddan-aram and his subsequent return to Canaan. Abraham and Isaac seem to have moved chiefly between two main areas, near Hebron (13: 18; 14: 13; 18: 1; 35: 27) and in the Negev (chs 20–21; 22: 19; 24: 62; 25: 11; 26: 6, 23; 28: 10). The sphere of Jacob's movements after his return from Paddan-aram was slightly further north, between Hebron and the region of Shechem (33: 18–19;

49

37: 12–14). These are in keeping with the way of life known as pastoral nomadism, requiring seasonal movements to meet the needs of the livestock. This will be explained more fully below.

Pastoral nomadism and settled life

One aspect of the patriarchs' lifestyle which strikes the careful reader·of the stories is their frequent contact with cities. Lot moved to settle near Sodom (Gen 13: 12) and later became an inhabitant of that city (14: 12; 19: 1). Abraham spent much time near Hebron (13: 18; 14: 13; 18: 1), and bought land from its inhabitants (ch 23). Abraham and Isaac both spent time settled in the vicinity of Gerar (20: 1; 26: 1–6), and both made a treaty with its king (21: 22–34; 26: 26–30). After his return from Paddan-aram, Jacob settled for a while near Shechem and bought land from its people (33: 18–19). The Shechemites pressed for a closer link with Jacob's group, including intermarriage, but the move ended in hostilities (34: 8–31). Nevertheless, we find Jacob pasturing his flocks near Shechem again on a later occasion (37: 12).

The nature of the links between the patriarchs and the cities is to be understood in terms of economic interdependence. The Old Testament shows the patriarchs to have been pastoralists, raising sheep and cattle (12: 16; 13: 7; 20: 14; 21: 27; 24: 35; 26: 14; 33: 17; 37: 12; 47: 1–6), and also having asses and camels (24: 10, 35 etc). However, there are also plenty of references to agricultural products in the narratives. Abraham was able to offer his guests cakes made from meal, as well as a calf (18: 6–7); Jacob bought Esau's birthright with bread and a stew of lentils (25: 29–34); Isaac drank wine with his meat (27: 25) and blessed Jacob with the promise of grain and wine (27: 28); Jacob sent a present of balm, honey, gum, myrrh, pistachio nuts and almonds to Joseph in Egypt (43: 11). Clearly, the patriarchs were dependent on a combination of pastoralism and farming. The climate of Palestine provides the background to this economic situation. As we saw in chapter 1, during the winter the rains make it possible to graze flocks and herds in the hilly areas, but during the long, dry summer the herdsmen return to the valleys and plains to find water and pasturage. This probably explains why Jacob's sons took their flocks from the Hebron hills to Shechem, seventy-five kilometres (forty-seven miles) north as the crow flies, and then a further thirty-five kilometres (twenty-two miles) to the plain of Dothan (37:12–17). The pit in which Joseph's brothers put him had no water in it (37:24), which suggests these movements were a response to the dry season.

Since most major cities lay in the valleys and plains, these seasonal movements were the chief factor which brought the patriarchs into contact with settled life. If they moved into land under the jurisdiction of a city, they had to reach agreements with its rulers over grazing and water rights. This explains the treaties which Abraham and Isaac made with the people of Gerar, where water rights were a particular bone of contention. However, Isaac's stay in Gerar was not simply seasonal; he moved there to escape a famine (Gen 26:1). He had previously been living at Beer-lahai-roi (25:11), a location evidently near Kadesh (Gen 16:14). When the famine struck, he had a choice of either moving south to Egypt (as Abraham had done) or trying to find a place to settle further north. When God commanded him not to go to Egypt (26:2), the region of Gerar was the logical choice. The area has unusually plentiful and stable ground water, and several springs. Isaac evidently stayed there throughout the winter season, instead of venturing into the upland grazing areas, and successfully harvested crops (26:12). It is significant that the repeated quarrels over newly-dug wells stopped as Isaac moved away from Gerar towards Beersheba (26:17–22); the herdsmen of Gerar could no longer claim that the wells were theirs on the basis of their ownership of the land.

The pastoralist's need for grazing-land probably explains why Jacob purchased land from the people of Shechem (Gen 33:18–19). This was either an alternative to, or in addition to, the kind of treaty which Abraham and Isaac had made with the ruler of Gerar.

City-dwellers actually benefitted from allowing pastoralists to use their fields as grazing-land during the summer. It is still a common practice in some areas of the Fertile Crescent today for herdsmen to graze their flocks in the stubble of harvested fields. The animals thus fertilize the fields for the following season. As well as this mutually beneficial arrangement, products are exchanged between the semi-nomadic and settled communities. It is significant that the people of Shechem offered Jacob open access to their land and *the opportunity to trade* (34:10). When the patriarchs were not able to grow their own agricultural produce, as

Isaac was at Gerar, they would have obtained such things by trade with the cities. They would have arrived in the settled areas just after the harvesting of the grain crops, and probably left soon after the autumn harvest, so they were able to obtain the whole range of agricultural produce. In return, they would have provided the city-dwellers with meat, skins and wool from their flocks and herds. (As we will see below, however, not all cities needed to trade for such products, since some had farming villages attached to them in which pastoralism was practiced.)

City-dwellers and pastoral nomads were therefore related economically. This relationship between the settled and semi-nomadic communities was a way of making the most of the land, given the climatic conditions of the Fertile Crescent. Pastoral nomadism in the East was not a step *towards* settled life, but actually something which developed *out of* the settled life of the towns and agricultural villages, to make more efficient land-use possible. It is therefore not surprising that Abraham came originally from a settled environment, or that Jacob was able to make the transition to life in an agricultural village while he lived in Paddan-aram. Settled life and pastoral nomadism were never completely separate.

Village life

Villages in Old Testament times were generally small settlements without defensive walls (Lev 25: 31; Ezek 38: 11). Several different Hebrew words are used for such settlements, one of them meaning literally 'daughters' (eg Num 21: 25). This is because, in certain periods, many villages were tied economically and politically to larger cities, and so were regarded as the daughter settlements of the city they depended on. Because of this political and economic arrangement, we often read of 'cities ('towns', NIV) with their villages' (Josh 15: 32–61 etc). These villages were evidently grouped around their parent city, scattered among the fields and pasture lands which belonged to it (Lev 25: 31). The inhabitants of the villages were the farming families which worked in the fields. Their activities will be described later in this chapter.

However, not all villages in Old Testament Palestine were linked with cities. During the period 1200–1050 BC over a hundred small settlements sprang up in the central hill country, many of them well away from large towns, and these must have been independent and economically more or less self-sufficient. It is from the archaeology of some of these settlements that we have our clearest picture of village life in Old Testament times. Two excellent examples are the villages at Khirbet et-Tell (often assumed to be the site of biblical Ai) and Raddana, about six and a half kilometres (four miles) to the west. Both flourished during the period 1200–1050 BC (ie the time of the judges), but many of the insights into village life which they provide are valid for the whole Old Testament period, and for satellite villages as well as independent settlements.

Villages varied enormously in size, but the one at Raddana was fairly typical. It had about fifty houses and covered two acres. Its population was probably about 200 people at the most. Some villages were smaller than this, but some were larger. The one at Khirbet et-Tell had about eighty houses covering two and three-quarter acres, and a population of perhaps 300. Few villages were bigger than five acres, and a village population would rarely have exceeded 500–600 people.

Village houses

The houses in the villages were small and very basic. Most houses at Khirbet et-Tell and Raddana were rectangular with only two or three rooms at ground level and a sleeping loft. Usually there was only one door, which led directly into the main room. To either the left or right of the doorway, a row of rough stone pillars separated the main room from a narrow side-room. Some houses had a third room running across the width of the house at the back (ie at the opposite end from the door). The main room often had a pit in the centre for a fire. This room was the living area and the place where meals were eaten. There was probably no furniture; people simply sat on the floor or on flat stones around the open fire. There was no separate kitchen. Instead, small ovens were located outside the door, often in a small courtyard shared by two or three houses.

In some houses at Khirbet et-Tell, access to the side-rooms was through arched passages less than a metre high. These side-rooms were almost certainly shelters for sheep and goats. In some

Drawing of a typical flat-roofed, courtyard house, of the 10th century BC, based on one excavated at Tell Qasile. (C Davey)

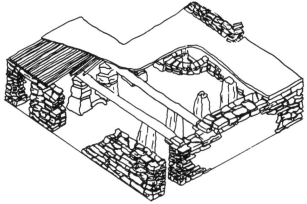

Pillar house at Khirbet et-Tell (Ai). This artist's reconstruction shows a basically simple rectangle, separated into two areas by a 'room divider' of roof support pillars. Beams rest on the pillars; across the beams are roof slats topped by white clay. In the far corner of the one-room house, a curved wall encloses a silo for storage jars of grain. The spaces between the stone piers on the left were once filled in, forming a wall with a second room behind it. This second room could be entered through the doorway at the far left.

settlements mangers have been found in the side-rooms, confirming this view. It is likely that the animals were brought into the houses at night, not just for their own protection but also because their bodies radiated warmth. It was probably usual for the sleeping loft to be situated above the shelter for the animals, to make the most of the warmth rising from their bodies. The smell from the animal shelter must have been very unpleasant at times, and we may assume that the villagers were far less bothered by odours than we are. A family of four or five probably slept together in the one sleeping loft. Poor peasant families would not have had beds; instead, they would have slept on matting, with their thick outer cloaks as their covering. In Exodus 22:26–7 we find a law that, 'If you ever take your neighbour's garment in pledge [for return of a loan], you shall restore it to him before the sun goes down; for that is his only covering, it is his mantle for his body; in what else shall he sleep?'

Many settlements had a slightly more elaborate design of house, now generally referred to as the 'four-room house'. In this type, the door led into a main 'room' (which some archaeologists think was actually an unroofed courtyard) of rectangular shape, the door being in one of the short sides. Narrow rooms ran parallel to this main room on both sides, with the fourth room spanning the width of the building at the back. As in the smaller houses, one of the side-rooms often served as a shelter for the animals, and the family probably slept in a loft above.

It is not always easy to estimate how much of a house was actual living space (as opposed to open courtyard, storage space or room for animals), but it is obvious that houses of both types were cramped by modern standards. The houses at Raddana probably provided an average of thirty-five square metres (forty-two square yards) of living space. Some settlements had larger houses with perhaps fifty-six square metres (sixty-seven square yards) of living space. It has been estimated that the smaller houses were home to about four people, and the larger ones to five or six people, allowing about ten square metres (twelve square yards) of living space per person. For comparison, a modern British house for the same number of people (eg a three-bedroom semi-detached) provides about eighty square metres (ninety-six square yards) of living space.

A typical Israelite house of the 'four-room' type: a central courtyard is surrounded on three sides by rectangular rooms. (In this case each is subdivided into smaller rooms: along the side with the roof cut away we can see a stable, kitchen and bedroom.) Some archaeologists believe the central court was roofed over, but others think it was an open courtyard. Some houses of this type had a loft above one of the side rooms. (C Davey)

Houses and the family unit

The typical family unit occupying a village house probably consisted of a father and mother and two or three children. (As we will see in ch 7, most marriages were probably monogamous after the time of the patriarchs – contrary to popular opinion.) Although couples would regularly have had more than two or three children, the infant mortality rate was probably high (as in many societies today where medical care is lacking), keeping most families small. It has been suggested that the infant mortality rate may have been as high as forty percent, and that perhaps thirty percent of the women died in childbirth. In families which enjoyed a low mortality rate for three or four generations, there could have been as many as twenty or thirty members. However, such families would have been the exception rather than the rule. Children were considered a great blessing (Ps 127:3–5), since they not only continued the family name (if male), but were also a source of labour in the home and the fields, and provided security for the parents in later life.

However, a single house does not give us the whole picture of family life. At Khirbet et-Tell and Raddana, as at many other places, the houses were arranged in compounds. Each compound consisted of usually three (sometimes two) houses and a shared courtyard. These compounds represent multiple (or extended) families, each with about a dozen members. A typical multiple family might consist of a father and mother, their married sons with their wives and children, as well as any unmarried brothers, sisters, sons and daughters of the original couple. There might also be a surviving great-grandparent in the family, making a total of four generations sharing the compound. The fact that three or even four generations lived connected lives probably explains biblical passages such as Exodus 20:5, where God speaks of punishment falling upon 'the children to the third and the fourth generation of those who hate me' (see Exod 34:7; Num 14:18; Deut 5:9). Such passages do not mean that the punishment will be extended over a long period of time, but that it will affect the entire household of the guilty party.

In a family of three generations the head of the household would have been the grandfather. In the event of his death, his married sons and their families may have remained together as a single household, in which case the head of the family would have been the eldest son. But some researchers believe that the household usually divided at such a time, each married son becoming the head of a new household.

Abraham's relatives in the vicinity of Haran probably lived in family compounds of this type in an agricultural village. The narrative certainly gives the impression that several near relatives lived in close proximity (Gen 24:28–29, 50). A clearer example is the household of Micah in Judges 17–18. Micah is evidently the head of the household, so his father must have died. He is a married man with adult sons, and his household contains his widowed mother and at least one of his sons (and that son's wife and family?). This much is clear from Judges 17:1-5. Micah then installs a young Levite as priest of the family shrine, and the Levite also becomes a member of the household (17:12). There were also other men in the household, perhaps brothers or other sons of Micah. They are mentioned in 18:22, which describes how, when a group of Danites took the Levite away from Micah's household, 'the men who were in the houses near Micah's house' (RSV) set out in pursuit. This phrase probably means 'the men who were in the houses comprising Micah's household', referring to a family compound.

Multiple families of this type, living in houses close together or even attached to each other, still exist in some Arab villages today. They are economic units as well as social units; that is, the multiple family collectively owns and farms the land from which it obtains its livelihood. It is for the compound that food is grown, processed, stored, prepared and served. This probably gives us a fairly good guide to the workings of similar family groups in Old Testament times. As we shall see in chapter 7, the multiple family (ie the family occupying a compound) was considered the basic unit of Israelite society.

Building materials and house construction

In hill country areas where stone is plentiful the walls of houses were built from large field-stones. No attempt was made to shape them to fit neatly together, so the gaps between them were filled with smaller stones. A daub of plaster or mud was applied to give a smooth appearance and to make the house warmer in winter. This would have needed regular repair to prevent cracks developing. Cracks or gaps between the stones must have provided homes for a multitude of insects and even lizards and snakes. A vivid image used by Amos is of a man who 'went into the house and leaned with his hand against the wall, and a serpent bit him' (Amos 5:19).

In the lowlands the common building material was mud-brick, that is, bricks of baked or sun-dried mud. Many villages in parts of the Near East today (especially in Egypt) have houses of mud-brick. In Old Testament times it was usual to lay a foundation of two or three layers of large stones and to erect the mud-brick walls on top of that.

Roofs were flat. Wooden roof-beams reached from wall to wall, supported by rough stone pillars (as at Khirbet et-Tell) or wooden poles. On top of these was placed a layer of thin branches covered with a thick mud plaster. There was probably easy access to the roof by means of steps or a ladder outside the house, since it needed replastering at least once a year to keep out the winter rains. A leaking roof was a common problem; the writer of Proverbs compares a quarrelsome woman with 'a continual dripping on a rainy day' (Prov 27: 15). Since careful maintenance was needed to keep the roof waterproof, Ecclesiastes remarks: 'Through sloth the roof sinks in, and through indolence the house leaks' (10: 18).

During the summer the roof was a convenient place to dry figs, raisins, flax etc (eg Josh 2: 6). The roof was generally low. Those at Khirbet et-Tell were so low that the villagers must have had to stoop constantly to avoid hitting their heads on the thick beams which supported them. Roof-beams and side walls had to be particularly strong where they also supported a second storey, ie the sleeping loft.

Windows were simply holes in the walls, sealed by shutters when necessary. They were kept to a minimum in order to keep the house as cool as possible in summer and as warm as possible in winter. Their main purpose was to let light in and smoke out, so they were set high in the walls. Floors were usually of beaten earth, though sometimes they were cobbled and sometimes a mixture of lime and mud was used as a plaster. Doorways consisted of a threshhold, two doorposts and a lintel. These components were sometimes of stone, sometimes of wood (Exod 21: 6). The door itself was made of wood, fixed to a wooden post which turned with it, rotating in a hollowed stone at the base and in a hole in the lintel at the top. Some doors could be bolted (2 Sam 13: 17–18).

The water-supply in a village usually consisted of cisterns cut out of the rock beneath the floors of the houses or their courtyards. (See ch 5 for more detail on cisterns.) The water available to each family was therefore very limited, and it was especially important to use it sparingly during the dry season. Water would have been used chiefly for drinking and boiling food. Personal hygiene was probably limited to washing hands and feet.

Village activities

The main activities of the villagers were agricultural. They worked in the surrounding fields, orchards and pastures, to which they moved out each morning, returning to the village at the end of the day (Judg 19: 16; Ps 104: 22–23).

The excavations at Khirbet et-Tell and Raddana produced several flint blades which had originally been the teeth of sickles, attached to a wooden haft. These sickles were probably used for harvesting cereals and also for cutting dry grass, which was used as kindling for the ovens (compare Luke 12: 28). Once harvested, grain was threshed by dragging a threshing-sledge over it, the sledge usually being pulled by oxen (2 Sam 24: 22). A flat area of exposed limestone made the ideal threshing floor, and such an area would have been shared by several farming families.

The remains of sheep and goats were also found at Khirbet et-Tell, showing that these villagers were pastoralists as well as farmers. The animal shelters in the houses have already been mentioned; the sheep and goats were brought back to the village at night to be sheltered in the houses, and also in enclosures on the edge of the village. Each morning they were taken out to fresh pasture, which sometimes involved a long trek.

In the hills, crops were grown on artificial terraces. Walls of rough stones were laid along the natural contours of the hills to retain the soil behind them, and the soil was levelled off to form a series of steps down the hillsides. In this way narrow, curving 'fields' were created, suitable for agriculture. Terrace-farming is still carried on today, and many existing terrace systems are renovations of those first created in Old Testament times. Terraces could be used for planting vineyards or olive groves, or for growing grain.

Before sowing, the soil was broken up and turned over with a simple plough. This would have had a single blade – of bronze, hardwood or (after 1000 BC) iron – and so could only have cut one furrow at a time. The animals used for pulling ploughs were oxen and asses, either singly or yoked together in pairs.

As well as farming and herding, there was also work to be done at home. Grain was ground to make flour, bread was baked, and other food cooked. Stones for grinding grain are commonly found in excavations and are of two main types. The saddle-quern was a large stone with a concave upper surface, against which the grain was ground with the aid of a smaller stone rubbed backwards and forwards. The other type was a stone mortar and pestle. Grain was stored in the house, usually in one corner of the room separated off by a low curved wall. The grain was kept in this space in large storage jars.

Ovens for baking bread were usually outside the houses in the courtyard, and were probably shared by the whole compound. A typical oven was a dome of clay or rough pottery, fifty or sixty centimetres (about two feet) in diameter at the base and about thirty centimetres (one foot) high. The fuel (sticks and charcoal with dry grass for kindling) was put in through an opening in one side. There was another aperture at the top and air-vents at the base. Flat cakes of dough were simply stuck to the sides and top of the oven until baked on one side, and then turned over to bake the other (Hos 7: 8).

The oven could also be used for cooking, by placing a cooking-pot over the top aperture. A cooking-pot could also be placed on a simple arrangement of stones with space for a fire in the centre. Some hearths of stones were quite large, and were obviously for communal use. Cooking-pots were pottery vessels with wide necks and either flat or rounded bases. They were commonly about thirty centimetres (one foot) in diameter and eighteen centimetres (seven inches) deep, though some were smaller. Some had holes just below the rim, and it has been suggested that this indicates the use of a lid, the holes being to let steam out. However, the holes could have been for string, woven in and out around the rim to form loops for handles. A boiling pot would certainly have been too hot to lift with bare hands. It is likely that most cooked food consisted of vegetables, meat being reserved for special feasts.

It seems that grinding grain, baking and cooking were traditionally the jobs done by women (Gen 18: 6; 27: 9; Exod 11: 5), as was weaving, which will be discussed in the next chapter. Work in the fields was generally done by men, but there was no firm demarcation. When more hands were needed in the fields, women worked there too (Ruth 2). The children of the villages would also have been involved in the daily tasks as soon as they were old enough to be useful.

Nightfall put a stop to all work, in the fields and in the village.

There were lamps for lighting the houses, but these gave only a candle-like flame, so the rooms were fairly dim places at night. A lamp was simply a small bowl for oil, with the rim pinched together at one side to form a rest for the wick (a piece of cloth). Nightfall was the time for the family to gather for a meal around the fire, for an exchange of news and gossip, and to prepare for sleep.

In the independent villages there were workshops for crafts such as pottery-making and metallurgy. One compound at Khirbet et-Tell had its own workshop where metal ingots were melted in crucibles and cast into moulds to make bronze daggers, axes and chisels. The metal ingots were one of the few things for which the villagers needed to trade. The one workshop probably served the whole village. The axes were perhaps used for felling trees. As we saw in chapter 1 the hill country was well wooded until settlements spread into the area, and clearance would have been necessary before the agricultural terraces were created. Larger trees would also have provided timber for house construction. Mature oak, terebinth, pine and cypress trees would have made ample roof-beams. The chisels were probably used for shaping the rough stone pillars which supported the roof-beams, and for cutting out cisterns.

Fewer crafts would have been carried out in those villages which were satellites to the large cities. They were economically dependent on their cities, the villagers obtaining their pottery, metal goods and other items in the city markets in exchange for agricultural produce. A satellite village also looked to its city for protection, and in times of military threat the villagers took refuge within its walls. Village life was therefore very vulnerable, and in a prolonged crisis it could almost disappear. Thus we read in the Song of Deborah that 'village life in Israel ceased' until Deborah led the tribes to victory over their enemies (Judg 5: 7, NIV).

CHAPTER FOUR

The Cities

There are some respects in which life in the cities was similar to that in the villages. The houses of the ordinary people were very like the village houses already described in terms of construction and layout, most being of the 'four-room house' design or variations on it. Family life for most city people was no different from our description of it in chapter 3. Even the wealthier households probably consisted of multiple families such as we have already described. However, it would seem that in better-off families the women had greater influence and responsibility (eg the ideal wife of Prov 31:10–31 is portrayed buying land on her own initiative, v 16).

There are therefore many features of city life which need not be described here, since they resembled those of village life. We will concentrate on describing those aspects of cities and city life which were distinctive. It should also be stressed that we are looking only at the cities of Israelite Palestine; the great cities of neighbouring lands such as Egypt and Mesopotamia were different in many respects, but we do not have space to describe them here.

City walls

Generally speaking, cities were distinguished not only by their size but by a surrounding wall. This was not always the case, however. During the Late Bronze Age (about 1500–1200 BC) there were relatively few fortified cities in Palestine (Megiddo, Gezer and Hazor were among them). Most were unwalled, but still distinguished from the villages by their size and by their temples and administrative buildings.

A city generally stood at some strategic point on a major route, and where a good source of water could be guaranteed. (On city water supplies, see ch 5.) The site was usually a small hill, making the city easier to defend against attack. As time went by, natural hills became enlarged by the accumulated debris of successive cities. This process will be described more fully below.

City walls varied in design and construction. It was common to have a foundation of large stones topped by a thick wall of mud bricks. The stone foundations of large fortification walls were massive affairs, sometimes built up above ground level, sometimes set in deep trenches. The walls themselves were very thick. A good example comes from Lachish, in the Shephelah. Lachish dominated north–south and east–west routes and in Hezekiah's day was second in importance only to Jerusalem among the cities of Judah. The city's main wall was six metres (nineteen feet) thick, built of brick on a stone foundation. The inner face (and perhaps the outer, too) was plastered over to produce a smooth surface. The remains of this wall still survive to a height of two metres (six feet) in places, and originally the wall must have been between two and three times that height, topped with ramparts. Beneath the foot of the main wall a glacis (an artificial sloping surface) was created, faced with a layer of stones. This extended about halfway down the hill on which the city stood, to where a second (ie outer) wall surrounded the city. This served as a retaining wall for the glacis, but also doubled as an extra line of defence. The outer wall was about four metres (thirteen feet) thick. The creation of such fortifications was obviously a massive engineering project.

While some city walls were solid, others were of the type known as 'casemate' walls. These consisted of two thinner walls with a space between, divided into chambers ('casemates') by short walls

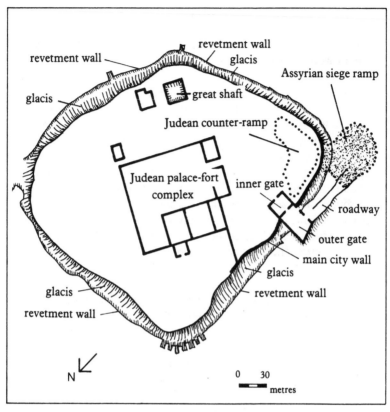

Plan of Lachish at the time of its siege by Sennacherib in 701 BC.

at right-angles. Sometimes these chambers within the wall served no purpose in themselves; they simply helped to create a wall of sufficient width for the top to be manned by defenders in case of attack. Sometimes, however, the casemate chambers formed the rear rooms of houses set around the inside of the wall. Rahab of Jericho had a house 'built into the city wall, so that she dwelt in the wall' (Josh 2:15). Walls were often built in sections which alternately jutted out or stood back from the main line of the wall. The sections which jutted out gave defending archers a wider arc of fire. Towers jutting out from the wall served the same purpose.

'Cities built on their mounds'

Despite their fortifications, cities frequently suffered destruction. This was not always the result of enemy attack, however. Earthquakes and accidental fires were other common causes. Because cities occupied strategic positions near roads and springs, a destruction did not usually result in the permanent abandonment of the site. Sooner or later, survivors or new settlers began the work of rebuilding. They would often salvage valuable materials such as hewn stones and use them again, but otherwise they simply built afresh on top of the ruins of the previous city. The ruins would commonly consist of mud-brick debris from collapsed buildings, in some places several feet thick. Therefore each time a city was destroyed and rebuilt, the new city stood slightly higher than its predecessor, being literally built on top of it. After many centuries of destruction and rebuilding, a city therefore stood on a sizeable mound of accumulated debris. The walls of cities contributed to the growth of such mounds. If an unwalled settlement was destroyed and abandoned for a time, it did not take long for the action of wind and rain to erode away the mud-brick remains. But a surrounding wall, even when reduced to a bank of rubble, helped to retain the layers of debris.

The Hebrew term for the ruin-mound of an ancient city is a *tel*. The Book of Joshua, recording Joshua's victory over the coalition of northern cities, relates that 'Israel did not burn any of the cities built on their mounds [*tels*] – except Hazor, which Joshua burned' (Josh 11:13, NIV). The word forms part of certain biblical place-names: Tel Melah, Tel Harsha (Ezra 2:59) and Tel Aviv (Ezek 3:15). All these are names of places in Babylonia where Jews were settled during the Exile, perhaps indicating that the exiles in those places had the task of rebuilding ruined towns. (The modern Tel Aviv, in Israel, was named after the Babylonian town in Ezek 3:15 and must not be confused with it.) When promising the return of the Jews to their own land and the restoration of Judah's cities, Jeremiah says: 'Every city shall be rebuilt on its mound of ruins' (Jer 30:18, NEB, where the last three words translate the Hebrew *tel*).

The related Arabic word, *tell*, occurs in the present-day names for the sites of numerous ancient cities (eg Tell Balata, Tell el-

Far'ah, Khirbet et-Tell, etc). Their mounds are visible today as flat-topped hills. By the careful excavation of these ruin-mounds archaeologists can piece together the history of an ancient city, since each layer of debris represents a period of occupation.

The city gate

The gate of a fortified city was naturally the weakest point in its defences. Gateways therefore tended to be elaborate affairs in an attempt to counteract this weakness. A gatehouse with rooms on either side of a central passageway is an arrangement found at a number of sites. The rooms were presumably guardrooms housing armed men. The gatehouse was flanked by tall towers on which watchmen could be posted and from which the gate could be defended by archers. The road leading up the slope of the mound usually approached the gate with the city wall to its right, so that a ninety-degree turn had to be made inside the gateway before entering the city. As well as making it more difficult for enemy forces to penetrate the gateway itself, this also forced attackers to approach the gate with their right sides (the side *not* defended by a shield) exposed to the archers on the city wall.

The gate of eighth-century BC Lachish provides an impressive example of this type of entrance. Lachish had a double gateway. The road up the slope of the mound led to the outer gate. This opened into a large rectangular enclosure which the British excavators of the 1930s called the Bastion. It was unroofed with a paved courtyard of over 600 square metres (720 square yards), with the outer gate in its southern side. In its eastern side stood the entrance to the inner gatehouse. This was a massive square structure covering an area of 612 square metres (734 square yards). Its entrance was flanked by towers where it joined the inner city wall. The gatehouse itself was roofed, with a passageway a little over five metres (sixteen feet) wide through the middle. There were three guardrooms on either side of the passageway, each about six metres (nineteen feet) long and three metres (ten feet) wide, divided by thick walls. Apparently only the outer end of the passageway was closed by doors. Fragments of these were found in the new excavations which began in 1973. Five pieces of bronze were

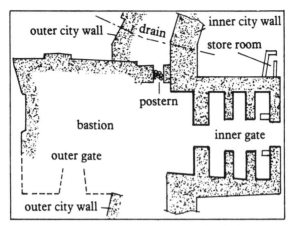

Plan of inner and outer gates at Lachish.

found, one having carbonized wood still attached to it. This has been identified as acacia, a hardwood suitable for strong and heavy doors. The actual design of the doors remains uncertain. It would seem (eg Isa 45: 1–2) that twin doors were common, meeting in the centre of the gateway when closed, and secured by a long beam or metal bar which spanned their combined width.

The inner gatehouse at Lachish is basically similar to gatehouses found at some other sites and also belonging to the time of the monarchy. Its size is exceptional, however. For example, the inner gatehouse at Megiddo, commonly dated to the reign of Solomon, was about eighteen metres (fifty-eight feet) wide and 20.3 metres (sixty-six feet) long, giving it an area of about 365 square metres (438 square yards); compare this with the 612 square metres (734 square yards) covered by the structure at Lachish.

The gate of a city played an important role in the social and economic life of its people. It was traditionally the place where all types of business were transacted (see eg Gen 23: 10, 18; Ruth 4: 1–12) and where legal cases were heard and settled by the judges and elders (see eg 2 Sam 15: 2–4; Job 29: 7–17; Prov 31: 23; Amos 5: 10–12, 15). It was consequently an area where public assemblies took place. In cities with a double gateway, like the one at Lachish, assemblies were probably held in the courtyard between the outer and inner gates. Otherwise the assembly area must have been immediately inside the city. As well as being the place for formal gatherings, the city gate must also have been a place to meet friends, watch traders coming and going, and catch up on news and gossip from beyond one's own city.

Sizes and populations

Like villages, the cities of Old Testament Palestine varied a great deal in size. But all were small compared with the modern cities of Europe and the USA. By modern western standards of size, most Old Testament cities were merely fortified villages. We need to remember this when trying to visualize any city of the biblical period.

The city of Lachish, whose walls and gate we have been describing, covered an area of about twenty acres during the time of the monarchy (ie the Iron Age). This was about average for an Old Testament city. Some were between five and ten acres in size, while others were much larger. During the Late Bronze Age, Shechem covered about twelve acres, Megiddo about fifteen and Gezer thirty. Some cities were even larger: Dan reached fifty acres, and Hazor had a *tell* of twenty-six acres and an adjacent area of a further 200 acres enclosed by a high earthen bank. By contrast Iron Age Hazor, built by Solomon (1 Kings 9: 15), consisted of only the western half of the *tell*.

As shown by the case of Hazor, many cities changed in size from time to time. The areas estimated by archaeologists for Jerusalem in different periods are an interesting reflection of its history. It is estimated that when David conquered the city from the Jebusites its area was about twelve acres. It increased to about thirty-two acres under Solomon, but its most dramatic increase came towards the end of the eighth century BC (the reign of Hezekiah) when it reached 125 acres. This probably indicates the migration to Jerusalem of refugees from the northern kingdom when Samaria fell to the Assyrians in 722 BC. After the Exile the city was very much smaller; the walls built by Nehemiah (Neh 2: 17–6: 15) enclosed about thirty acres, slightly less than the city of Solomon's day.

Population figures can be estimated on the basis of known areas. It is now generally assumed that the population density of cities in

Old Testament times was between 160 and 200 people per acre. Hence Lachish probably had a population of 3500–4000 during the monarchy; Late Bronze Age Shechem perhaps had about 2000 inhabitants, Megiddo 3000, Gezer 6000, Dan 10,000 and Hazor 40,000. However, Hazor's population was probably only 3000 in the time of Solomon. Jerusalem's population probably increased from about 2000 in the time of David to 5000 under Solomon, rising abruptly to 20–25,000 in the reign of Hezekiah, then dropping to 4500 in the post-exilic period.

For comparison with the above figures, the modern English town of Bristol covers about 27,500 acres and has a population of over 390,000. (These figures date from 1981.) There is not only an enormous difference in area and population but also in population *density* in comparison with an ancient city. Bristol has, on average, only about fifteen people per acre, compared with the 160–200 per acre estimated for ancient cities. Even a modern American city with many high-rise blocks has only fifty to eighty people per acre. One reason for this striking difference is that modern cities have a great deal of open space in them: most houses have their own gardens, and there are public parks and sports grounds. There are also large shopping centres and office blocks where many people work but none actually *live*. Our road systems also occupy considerable space. All these things were missing from the cities of the Old Testament world, and houses were relatively small and packed closely together.

Town plans and public buildings

Although some cities show little evidence of deliberate planning in the layout of their buildings, a basic town plan has now been detected at a number of excavated sites. At Beersheba, Tell en-Nasbeh (biblical Mizpah), Beth-shemesh and Tell Beit Mirsim a roughly similar plan has been identified, in each case dating from the time of the monarchy. In these cases the town was surrounded by a casemate wall (already described above), in which the casemate chambers formed the rear rooms of houses. These houses were generally of the simple four-room type or variations of it. This arrangement produced a ring of houses around the outer edge of the city, their rear walls being also the city wall (and consequently much thicker than the others). Within this ring of houses was a 'road' which ran all the way round the central core of the city. This 'road' was between two and five metres (between six and sixteen feet) in width. Within the central area enclosed by the road were more houses packed tightly together, intersected by narrow streets.

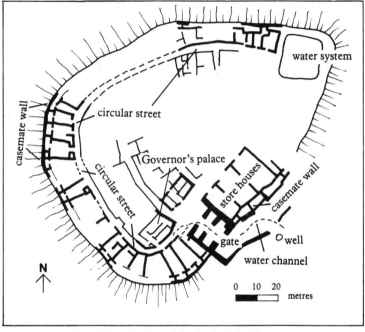

Town plan of Israelite Beersheba in the 9th–8th centuries BC.

Some cities seem to have consisted simply of houses (though many of those will also have functioned as workshops and shops), but others evidently played an important administrative role, since they had large public buildings in the central core or near the gate. A variety of such buildings have been excavated: governors' palaces, administrative buildings, storerooms and stables. At Beersheba in the eighth century BC a large building stood to the left of the city gate, and this was probably the residence of the local governor. To the right of the gate were three connected buildings which the excavators identified as storehouses. Each of these consisted of three long halls divided by two rows of stone pillars. The pillars had holes in them for the tethering of horses or asses, and stone mangers stood next to the pillars for the animals to feed from. The interpretation of the excavators is that the animals were tethered here while burdens were being loaded or unloaded from their backs. It is thought that the storerooms held a variety of goods (probably grain, wine and olive oil), and that a city with such buildings is what the Old Testament means by a 'store-city' (eg 1 Kings 9: 19; 2 Chron 16: 4). However, this view is challenged by other archaeologists, who argue that buildings of the kind found at Beersheba were actually *stables*. Similar buildings have also been excavated at Megiddo, Hazor and Lachish. Compelling arguments are offered by both sides and it is difficult to decide between them.

Some cities definitely had large communal granaries, but these were not in buildings of the kind described above. They were storage pits in the ground, lined with stones. Megiddo had a pit of this type, seven metres (twenty-three feet) deep, eleven metres (thirty-six feet) in diameter at the top, tapering to eight metres (twenty-six feet) at the bottom. Two sets of steps wound around the sides, giving access right to the bottom. This pit had a capacity of about 46,500 litres. It dates from the eighth or seventh centuries BC. A similar pit, dating from the tenth or ninth centuries BC, was discovered in the precincts of the governor's residence at Beth-shemesh. This measured seven metres (twenty-three feet) across the top and was six metres (nineteen feet) deep. Huge silos of this kind probably served a whole city. The collection of grain and its distribution must have been under the jurisdiction of the governor.

An outstanding example of a governmental building has been excavated at Lachish. This underwent a number of changes between the tenth and eighth centuries BC, and by the eighth century BC it was a very impressive building. It stood slightly to the west of the centre of the city, on a raised platform of large stones. Only the foundations have survived, but the superstructure was probably built of mud-brick. The main building, described as the palace-fort by the excavators, was rectangular, measuring seventy-six metres by thirty-six metres (247 feet by 117 feet). A building annexed to its northern end measured about thirty metres by thirty-six metres (97 feet by 117 feet). Connected with the palace-fort at its southern end, but aligned at right-angles to it, was another rectangular building, about sixty-two metres by twenty metres (200 feet by 65 feet). This building and the annex at the northern end served as either storehouses or stables. Perhaps in the case of Lachish there is some biblical evidence in favour of assuming these buildings were stables: we read in Micah 1:13: 'Harness the steeds to the chariots, inhabitants of Lachish' – implying that Lachish was equipped with horses and chariots for the defence of Judah's southwestern borders. Bounded by the palace-fort on the west and the storehouse or stables on the south was a huge lime-paved courtyard. This was enclosed by walls on the east and north, and measured about 100 metres by 60 metres (325 feet by 195 feet). The whole compound covered a total of three acres – about the size of a medium-to-large village! It was entered through a gateway in the southern rectangular building. This gateway faced a road which led in a straight line to the inner gatehouse of the city gate, already described.

Large governmental buildings such as the one at Lachish are probably the type of building referred to in the Old Testament by the Hebrew term 'armôn. Unfortunately English Bibles use a variety of words to translate this term: stronghold, fortress, citadel, palace, etc (eg 1 Kings 16:18; 2 Kings 15:25; Ps 48:13; Prov 18:19; Jer 9:21; Amos 3:9–11).

Rich and poor

Within the cities of the monarchic period (and also in some earlier Canaanite cities) there are clear signs of differences between the living conditions of the rich and the poor. The book of Amos indicates that in ninth century BC Israel the gulf between the rich and poor was very great. The poor had become the victims of injustice and exploitation by the influential rich. Archaeology confirms that major social differences arose under the monarchy, in contrast to the relative equality reflected by the material remains from the period of the judges.

Cities generally had many small houses of the kind already described in our account of village life (ch 3). For the families in such houses, living conditions were very like those of the villagers. A likely difference is that relatively few city people would have been engaged in agriculture. Most were probably involved in crafts and industries, which will be described below. Some city houses, although of basically the traditional four-room plan, were larger and better built than most, sometimes with a number of extra rooms added. These were presumably the houses of the more prosperous. Many of the better-off families, though not necessarily farmers themselves, owned land farmed by others (Prov 31: 16).

Occasionally we have clear evidence of the stark contrasts referred to by Amos. A striking example is provided by the eighth-century houses at Tell el-Far'ah, probably the site of biblical Tirzah, northeast of Shechem. In one part of the town the houses were substantial, built of hewn stones with dressed facings, the walls having well-fitted corners. These houses also had paved courtyards. Here the wealthy lived. Separated from this quarter by a wall were the dwellings of the poor. These were small, densely packed and makeshift in construction. Here we have a 'visual aid' to Amos's condemnation of the wealthy who 'trample upon the poor' and 'turn aside the needy in the gate' while building for themselves 'houses of hewn stone' (Amos 5: 11–12).

Amos also refers to those who had both a 'winter house' and a 'summer house' (Amos 3: 15). Evidently some of the rich could afford two houses, one located where it would catch cooling breezes during the summer, the other situated to avoid the worst weather of winter. The same verse mentions the 'houses of ivory', which doubtless means (as in the NIV's rendering) 'houses adorned with ivory' (see also Ps 45: 8). Again, these were the houses of the very wealthy. The kind of ivory adornments referred to have been found in the remains of the royal residence at Samaria, where Ahab is said to have built an 'ivory house' (1 Kings 22: 39). These are mostly plaques carved in open fretwork or low relief, often in designs with an Egyptian flavour. They were originally inlays, either for wooden wall-panels or for furniture. Furniture was a feature of the houses of the rich. The wealthy woman who provided a lodging-place for Elisha had it furnished with a bed, a table, a chair and a lamp (2 Kings 4: 8–10). Even among the wealthy, furniture would usually have been practical rather than luxurious. Amos, however, refers to the extravagant luxury in which the rich of Samaria lived (Amos 6:4):

> Woe to those who lie upon beds of ivory [ie beds decorated with ivory inlays], and stretch themselves upon their couches . . .

Those reduced to poverty by misfortune or the corrupt dealings of the rich must have lived lives of abject misery. The tragedy of the utterly destitute is described vividly in Job 24:5-12.

Crafts and industries

There is no doubt that the cities were the homes of competent craftsmen. We have room here to describe only some of the crafts and industries which were city-based.

The pottery industry

The pottery industry was probably the most widespread industry in Palestine throughout the biblical period, for two reasons. One is that there is plenty of suitable clay in Palestine, so pottery could be produced almost anywhere, provided there was a market for it. Secondly, pottery was in widespread use. Pottery vessels were used for the storage, preparation and serving of food and so were in constant use in every home. It has been estimated that household vessels lasted only one or two years before breaking, so with several vessels in regular use in every household, there was a constant demand for replacements.

From about 2000 BC pottery was made on a 'fast wheel', of which there were two forms. The simplest is known as the 'simple wheel' or 'hand wheel'. This was mounted on stone bearings. The lower bearing was a stone with a socket in the centre, fixed to the ground or a firm bench. The upper bearing was a stone with a projection which rotated in the socket. Attached to the upper bearing was a large disk of wood. This was both the potter's working platform and the flywheel of the apparatus. An assistant spun the disk by hand while the potter shaped his vessels on it.

A compound or double wheel (or 'kick wheel') came into use around 1300 BC or earlier and both types were widely used thereafter, right through the Iron Age and beyond. In the double wheel the working platform was a small wooden disk at the top end of a vertical wooden shaft. The bottom end of the shaft was fitted to a large flywheel which rotated on stone bearings of the sort already described. The flywheel was thus near the ground, so the potter could sit on a stool and work his vessel while kicking the flywheel round with his feet. This spun the shaft and the working platform. The book of Ecclesiasticus (or the Wisdom of ben Sirach), written around 180 BC, speaks of

> the potter sitting at his work and turning the wheel with his feet; he is always deeply concerned over his work, and all his output is by number (Sirach 38: 29, RSV Apocrypha).

Egyptian potters can still be seen operating wheels of this sort today.

When a vessel had reached its proper shape it was left to dry to a leathery hardness. Then, if required, it was dipped in a watery clay solution (a 'slip') to seal the pores and improve its finish. Sometimes pots were burnished by being rubbed smooth with a pebble. Some pots were decorated with a painted design or a pattern scratched onto the surface. During the time of the monarchy, painted decoration was extremely rare, though it had previously been common.

Finally, a whole batch of pots were fired together in a kiln, a process which took several days. Kilns consisted basically of two chambers: the hearth or fire-chamber, and a separate chamber in which the pots were placed. In a vertical type of kiln, such as was commonly used throughout the Late Bronze and Iron Ages, the pottery chamber was above the fire-chamber, the pots being stacked on a perforated floor which allowed the hot air and gases to rise. Horizontal kilns were also used, in which the pottery chamber and fire-chamber were side by side.

A very well preserved vertical kiln has been found at the Phoenician city of Sarepta (biblical Zarephath), dating from the thirteenth century BC. In this example the fire-chamber was oval and below ground level. It measured 2.4 metres by 1.85 metres (eight feet by six feet) and was 1.3 metres (four feet) deep. Its walls were lined with clay. The partition floor between this and the pottery chamber above was also of clay, about thirty to forty cm (twelve to fifteen inches) thick, with over thirty vents in it. Some vents were found closed with stones – evidently a way of controlling the heat. The upper part of the pottery chamber had not survived, but it was probably a large clay dome with a closable entrance at one side and a hole at the top to serve as a chimney. Three kilns of the horizontal type have been found at Tell en-Nasbeh (biblical Mizpah), north of Jerusalem.

A number of potters' workshops have been found in Palestine. These tend to be on the outskirts of the cities, probably because this gave the potters easier access to their sources of clay, and also because the smoke from their kilns would have been a great irritant in the confines of the city itself. Caves made ideal workshops because they were cool in summer and relatively warm and dry in winter, and also because they were excellent drying places for freshly turned vessels. While pots are drying to leathery hardness before firing, all parts have to dry at the same rate to avoid cracking. Hence they must be protected from draughts and direct sunlight.

The most extensive area of pottery workshops found in Palestine is one at Megiddo, where potters occupied caves on the eastern slope of the mound. This was a pottery workshop area during both the Late Bronze Age and the Iron Age. The pottery workshop area found at Sarepta was in use in the same periods, for a total of about 1000 years. Twenty-two vertical kilns (one of which has already been described) were located at the northwest corner of the Sarepta site. Jerusalem probably had a potters' quarter in the time of the monarchy. We are not told the location of 'the potter's house' mentioned in Jeremiah 18: 1–3, but Jeremiah subsequently bought 'a potter's earthen flask' which he smashed as a symbolic gesture 'at the entry of the Potsherd Gate', evidently on the southern side of the city in the valley of Hinnom or Topheth (Jer 19: 1–13). The Potsherd Gate was probably so-named because it led out to the place where the potters worked and where they dumped their broken vessels. It must have been common for pots to break during firing, since it would have been difficult to maintain steady temperatures in the kilns.

It is clear from the workshop areas discovered by archaeologists that pottery was mass produced and its manufacture was not a home industry (except in self-sufficient villages). It has been suggested that the potters of ancient Palestine were organized into guilds (see 1 Chron 4:23). This would certainly be in keeping with their workshops being clustered together. Individual workshops were probably run by families which maintained the tradition for several centuries. The potters would either have sold their wares directly to consumers at the city's market, or to itinerant merchants who sold pottery over wide areas, travelling from village to village.

It seems likely that other crafts and industries in the cities were organized in a similar way to the pottery industry. The existence of guilds for various crafts is implied by references to 'the families of the house of linen workers at Beth-ashbea' in 1 Chronicles 4:21 and 'the valley of craftsmen' at Ono in Nehemiah 11:35; Jerusalem had its 'street of the bakers' (Jer 37:21) and its groups of perfume-makers (Neh 3:8) and goldsmiths (Neh 3:31–32).

Metalworking

Metalworking was carried out extensively, as shown by the many biblical references to it and by archaeological finds.

Craftsmen in the cities would have obtained their raw materials in the form of metal bars (ingots) from itinerant traders. Copper and iron were mined in Palestine itself (Deut 8:9), but it is likely that the local sources had to be supplemented by imports. Cyprus was probably the main supplier of copper, while iron may have come from Anatolia via the Phoenician ports (Ezek 27:12, 19). Palestine's local copper was mined chiefly in the southern part of the Arabah. Copper mining and smelting installations dating from several periods have been found there, notably at Timna. These include shafts and tunnels which bring to mind Job's vivid description of mining ventures:

Man puts an end to the darkness;
he searches the farthest recesses
for ore in the blackest darkness.
Far from where people dwell he cuts a shaft . . .
far from men he dangles and sways. . .
He tunnels through the rock;
his eyes see all its treasures (Job 28:3–4, 10, NIV).

Copper alloyed with a small percentage of tin produced bronze.

The great advantage of bronze over copper was that it could be cast, making mass-production possible. Bronze is also a harder metal than copper. Copper could be hardened by hammering, but the resulting temper was not permanent. Bronze was therefore more suitable than copper for tools and weapons. Credit for the first extensive use of bronze goes to the Sumerians of southern Mesopotamia, who perfected the technique of alloying copper with tin around 3000–2700 BC. In Palestine bronze replaced copper soon after 2000 BC. The tin required to make bronze was not widely available, and the sources used by the metalsmiths of the ancient Near East are still not known for certain. Possibly they included northeast Anatolia and Trans-Caucasia. It seems likely that the bronze used in Palestine arrived there ready-made as ingots. We have already noted (ch 3) that bronze ingots were found in the metal workshop at Khirbet et-Tell. David obtained large quantities of bronze (probably as ingots) through his conquests of the Aramean states (1 Chron 18:8). Ezekiel refers to bronze being imported through the Phoenician city of Tyre (Ezek 27:13).

Although iron ore is very widespread, iron was the last of the common metals to be produced. This is because it was difficult to separate it from its oxides using ancient techniques. Iron does not melt below 1537° C, whereas ancient furnaces were not capable of producing temperatures above about 1200°. However, it was discovered that iron could be produced by a complicated *double* smelting process, and iron objects were being manufactured by about 1400 BC, and perhaps earlier. It was subsequently discovered that when iron is heated with charcoal the result is a product even harder than bronze. So from about 1200 BC (the date which is taken to mark the start of the Iron Age) iron began to replace bronze for the manufacture of tools and weapons. Iron did not come into common use in Palestine until after 1000 BC. Then it was used to make a wide variety of items: agricultural implements (1 Sam 13:20–21), weights (1 Sam 17:7), nails and fittings for wooden doors (1 Chron 22:3) and bars for fastening city gates (Isa 45:2). It was also used for weapons: iron axes, daggers and arrowheads have been found in excavations.

Gold was not found in Palestine but was mined in Egypt and Arabia. Much gold was obtained from Ophir (1 Kings 9:28; 1 Chron 29:4, etc), which was probably an Arabian locality (see also 2 Chron 9:14). Ezekiel refers to Tyre also receiving gold from Arabian traders (Ezek 27:21–22). Silver was mined in Anatolia and the mountains bordering the Red Sea, and Solomon obtained it from the Arabs (2 Chron 9:14). A gold ingot and an amount of silver were among the items stolen by Achan from the spoil of Jericho (Josh 7:21). Silver ore regularly contained impurities which were removed by smelting. At high temperatures, molten lead and other impurities sink and the lighter silver comes to the surface and can be skimmed off. Jeremiah refers to this process for purifying silver, using it as a metaphor for God's attempts to purify Israel (Jer 6:29–30; see also Prov 17:3; Ezek 22:17–22; Zech 13:9). From very early periods gold and silver were used to make jewellery (eg Exod 3:22; 11:2, etc) and luxury household items (cups, bowls and plates). Both precious metals were worked by beating, soldering, engraving and the filigree technique. Thin sheets of beaten gold were used extensively as overlays in Solomon's temple (1 Kings 6:20–35), a practice known also from Egyptian temples.

Ingots acquired by the craftsmen were melted down and the molten metal poured into moulds. The tools of the trade have been found at a number of sites. A typical furnace for smelting was beehive-shaped with air-holes near the bottom for a draught. Bellows were used to heat the furnace to sufficiently high temperatures (Isa 54:16; Jer 6:29). The fuel for the furnaces was charcoal. The metal was smelted in earthenware crucibles and cast in moulds, either of limestone or clay. Moulds for figurines, weapons, tools and items of jewellery have been found widely in excavations.

As in the case of pottery, the metalsmith's products were probably sold at the local markets or to middle-men, itinerant traders who sold them in turn throughout towns and villages over a wide area.

Weaving

Clothes were made from either wool or linen. Linen was produced from flax by a process illustrated in Egyptian tomb paintings. These show how flax was grown and depict the stages involved in turning the fibres into yarn and weaving the yarn into cloth. Flax was grown in Palestine (Josh 2:6 etc) and linen garments were manufactured (1 Chron 4:21; Prov 31:24), but wool from sheep and goats was much more widely available and so was more commonly used.

When the sheep and goats had been shorn the wool was first washed and bleached. This was the work of the fuller. The process involved cleaning the wool in an alkaline solution (the 'fuller's soap' used as a symbol of God's purifying activity in Mal 3:2) made with saltpetre or potash, and it would have produced a very unpleasant smell. We read of a 'highway to the Fuller's Field' somewhere on the southeastern side of Jerusalem (Isa 7:3; 36:2), which suggests there was a traditional area where the bleaching process was carried out, well away from the city because of the smell.

The wool was then spun (Exod 35:25–26) on a spindle using a distaff (Prov 31:19). The method was probably similar to that found among Bedouin women today. If so, the spindle was a rod about a metre long with one or two weights at the end to keep it steady while it was being turned. The fibres of wool were placed on the distaff in a ball. The distaff was then held under the left arm and the spindle in the left hand. The right hand was used to draw fibres from the distaff onto the spindle, which was skilfully turned at great speed. This spun the fibres into yarn.

If required, the yarn was then dyed. Purples, reds and blues seem to have been popular colours for quality clothes and hangings (see 2 Chron 2:7; Prov 31:19–24). Some stone vats excavated at Tell Beit Mirsim have been interpreted as a dye-plant, with the implication that Tell Beit Mirsim had a large wool-dying industry. However, this has recently been questioned and the vats re-interpreted as olive-presses (on which see below).

When the dyed yarn was dry it was ready for weaving. Wooden-framed hand-looms were used, and these could be either horizontal or vertical. Bedouin women still use simple horizontal looms today, to weave the considerable lengths of goats-hair fabric from which Bedouin tents are made. Vertical looms were also used in biblical Palestine. These consisted of two vertical posts with a horizontal cross-piece at the top. The warp threads were fastened to the cross-piece and held straight by a weight attached to the end of each one. Stone loom-weights have been found in excavations at dozens of sites in Palestine. The horizontal threads (the woof) were woven under and over the warp threads with a rod of wood or bone. This was the weaver's shuttle. A skilled weaver could use the shuttle with great speed, giving rise to Job's despairing remark: 'My days are swifter than a weaver's shuttle' (Job 7:6). The weaving was done at the top of the loom and the woven fabric rolled onto the horizontal cross-piece. This was the 'weaver's beam' to which the shaft of Goliath's spear is compared (1 Sam 17:7).

It is clear from Exodus 35:25–26 and Proverbs 31:19 that spinning and weaving were traditionally done by women, as is still the case among the Bedouin today. It also seems, to judge from the distribution of loom-weights at excavated sites, that weaving was a home-based industry, in contrast to pottery-making and metal-working. However, garments of wool and linen were not produced solely for the household; an efficient wife could make enough to sell to travelling merchants at the market (Prov 31:24).

Stonemasons and carpenters

Skilled stonemasons will have been involved in the construction of the larger buildings for which hewn stone was used. Limestone is widely available in Palestine, producing buildings of a pleasant pale honey colour. Many ancient quarries have been found, and from the surviving traces of ancient techniques we can reconstruct the method by which large blocks of limestone were removed. Rows of holes were bored in the rock and wooden wedges were then inserted in them. When these were soaked with water they expanded, splitting off large blocks of stone. These were further cut and shaped using chisels. Solomon obtained stone for the temple from quarries in the central hill country (1 Kings 5:15). The monumental gateways and decorated capitals found in excavations of the monarchic period testify to the fine skills of the Israelite craftsmen.

As well as quarrying and building, stonemasons must have been employed to excavate tombs, water-tunnels (see ch 5), and communal cisterns and grain-silos. (Small domestic cisterns were probably cut by the householders themselves.)

Carpenters will have been employed on larger buildings, where specialist knowledge was needed for the construction of roofs and doors. The manufacture of the massive doors for city gates must have involved both carpenters and metalsmiths. Furniture for wealthier households, chariots, carts, yokes and various farm implements also called for the skills of a specialist carpenter.

Agricultural industries

Although farming was primarily done by villagers, much of their produce found its way to the cities for storage and processing. We saw above how Megiddo and Beth-shemesh had large grain-storage facilities. Other cities were centres for wine-making and olive-oil production.

As we saw in chapter 1, grapes were grown plentifully in biblical Palestine and wine was the most common drink of the period (perhaps even more commonly drunk than water, which was prone to contamination). Wine production involved many people at different levels. The grapes were trodden in the presses with bare feet to extract the juice (Isa 63:3; Amos 9:13). The presses were large, shallow basins hewn out of the rock. The grape harvest was a time of rejoicing, and people often sang as they trod the fruit (Jer 48:33). However, it was sometimes a job done by the poor for wealthy landowners who gave them little reward (Job 24:11).

Juice flowed from the presses into pits in the rock. These had outlets above the base of the pit, so that pips and skin could settle out while the juice flowed on into collecting vats. These were more basins hewn out of the rock (Isa 5:2). The wine was then put in jars or skins for fermentation. Fermenting wine produces gases, so new wine had to be stored in new skins which could stretch as the process went on (see Job 32:19). Old skins were useless for new wine, because they had already stretched and so would split as the gases built up inside (hence Jesus' remark in Luke 5:37–38).

At the site of Gibeon an extraordinary complex of sixty-three wine cellars was discovered, cut into the limestone bedrock. These were in use at the time of the late monarchy. Each cellar was a pear-shaped chamber about two metres deep with a narrow entrance at the top. They contained large pottery jars, each having a capacity of forty-five litres. It has been calculated that the total capacity of the sixty-three cellars, fully stocked with jars, would have been about 95,000 litres (25,000 gallons). This is far more wine than the people of Gibeon could have used, so wine was obviously stored here for sale and distribution to other places. The Gibeon wine cellars therefore imply the existence of a complex bureaucracy to administer the collection, storage, sale and distribution of wine.

The crushing of olives to yield olive oil was another important industry. Olive oil was widely used in lamps and for cooking, and so was an important commodity. Olive presses have now been found at several places.

There were two main stages to the process. The preliminary crushing of the olives was done in a variety of ways. One involved placing the olives in a large, circular stone basin. A thick wheel of stone with a long wooden handle fixed in its centre was then rotated (either by manpower or animals) so that it rolled over the olives and squeezed out the oil. Channels cut in the stone allowed the oil to be drained off and collected. The oil from this first crushing was considered especially pure; this was the 'clear oil of pressed olives' used for lamps in the tabernacle and the temple (Exod 27:20; Lev 24:2, NIV).

The second stage was designed to extract all the remaining oil from the crushed olives. They were removed from the stone basin and placed in woven baskets, and the baskets were then stacked on a stone which was hollowed out to catch the oil. The baskets of olive pulp were then squeezed. First a large stone was placed on top of the baskets, and across the top of this rested a wooden beam. One end of the beam pivoted in a socket in the back wall of the installation. The other end was weighted by having large stones hung from it. The beam thus became a lever for pressing out the oil from the pulp in the baskets. However, the oil produced by this second stage was not so pure as that obtained by the first stage. The oil flowed from a channel in the stone beneath the baskets, to a vat or a collecting jar set in a hollow.

Olive-press complexes have been discovered at Gezer, Beth-shemesh and Tell Beit Mirsim. As noted above, some installations at Tell Beit Mirsim have been identified as dye-vats, but there seems to be a stronger likelihood that all the installations were olive-presses. At Dan an installation has been discovered in a sanctuary area. It is not surprising to find an olive-press associated with a sanctuary, because olive oil was used in several ritual activities. As noted already, oil from the first crushing was used in the lamps of the tabernacle and temple; cereal offerings were mixed with oil (Exod 29:40 etc), and it was used in anointing rituals (Exod 29:7; 30:23-33, etc).

Many of the crafts and skills described in this chapter must have been practiced widely, not just by specialists in the cities. We have already seen that weaving was a widespread home industry. We also saw earlier that the houses of villagers and most townspeople were of simple construction, consisting of mud-brick or uncut field-stones with roofs of wood and clay; these were not the work of specialist craftsmen, but were built and maintained by the families who lived in them. Most families probably excavated their own household cisterns and made and repaired the simpler agricultural tools. In the self-sufficient villages even pottery-making and metallurgy were probably widespread skills, though practiced on a fairly small scale. It was in the cities, however, that the mass-production of pottery and metal goods went on, and where olive oil production and the storage of grain and wine happened on a large scale. This reflects the role of the cities in the economic and administrative organization of the country in Old Testament times. We will discuss this further in chapter 8.

CHAPTER FIVE

Water

Most readers of this book will be living in a western country where a constant supply of clean water is taken for granted. It requires some effort to imagine the very different conditions of the biblical world, where people could depend on neither the constancy nor the cleanliness of their water-supply. Recurrent droughts and famines in parts of Africa should remind us, however, of how vital water is for life, and of the tragedy which results when water fails. Unless we can appreciate how basic water was to all aspects of life in Old Testament times, we miss the importance of a great deal of the Bible's imagery. Rainfall was seen as literally a token of God's goodness, and water is often symbolic of spiritual blessing and refreshment (eg Ps 23: 2; Isa 12: 3; 35: 6–7; 41: 17–18; Hos 6: 3). A lack of water was one of the most serious things that could happen, and was interpreted by the prophets as God's rebuke to his people (1 Kings 17: 1; Jer 14: 1–9; Joel 1: 15–20; Amos 4: 7–8; Hag 1: 11).

There were basically six sources of water in Old Testament Palestine: rainfall, dew, springs, streams, wells and cisterns. If this list creates the impression that water was abundantly available, we should remember that not one of these sources could be relied upon totally. We will look at each in turn.

Rain and dew

Moses described Palestine to the Israelites as 'a land of hills and valleys which drinks water by the rain from heaven' (Deut 11: 11), in sharp contrast to Egypt, where their plots of land had been irrigated with water from the Nile. However, as we saw in chapter 1, rainfall in Palestine is seasonal, the rainy season beginning in October and ending in April. From May to October no rain falls at all. During this hot, dry summer many areas become completely parched, and in Old Testament times the autumn rains were looked forward to with eagerness. A failure of the autumn rains prolonged the dryness of summer into a drought which threatened crops, animals and people alike. Jeremiah describes such a drought (Jer 14: 4–6):

> There is no rain on the land,
> the farmers are ashamed,
> they cover their heads.
> Even the hind in the field forsakes her newborn calf
> because there is no grass.
> The wild asses stand on the bare heights,
> they pant for air like jackals;
> their eyes fail because there is no herbage.

There were also serious consequences if the rainy season did not last all the way through to the end of April. This prevented the ripening of the barley and wheat, which (as we saw in ch 1) were harvested in May–June. The prophet Amos refers to a situation when the rains stopped in February, 'when there were yet three months to the harvest' (Amos 4: 7), and Joel describes the effect of a similar situation on crops and animals (Joel 1: 17–20):

> The seed shrivels under the clods,
> the storehouses are desolate;
> the granaries are ruined
> because the grain has failed. . .
> Even the wild beasts cry to thee
> because the water brooks are dried up.

A failure of the grain harvest naturally meant the threat of famine later on. A shortened rainy season also meant that many people could not collect enough water to get them through the long dry summer.

Apart from human efforts at water-storage and irrigation, crops which grow during the summer months are dependent on dew. Dew is formed when water-vapour condenses. This condensation can happen either on a surface, as when drops of dew form on the ground or on plants; or in the air, which produces mist. Both these things occur during the nights of Palestine's long, dry summer, and both are beneficial to the growth of crops. Dew-fall in Palestine depends on moist air drawn in from the Mediterranean, and is therefore heaviest near the coast and on the western side of the central hill country. Dew is estimated to fall for 250 nights of the year along the coast and on Mount Carmel, but for only 100–150 nights of the year in the Judean hills, decreasing rapidly as one approaches the Jordan valley. Because the greatest amounts fall during the summer, the dew compensates for the lack of rain.

The importance of dew for the ripening of summer crops was well appreciated in Old Testament times, and there are plenty of references to it (eg Gen 27:28; Deut 33:28; 2 Sam 17:12; Job 29:19; 38:28; Isa 18:4; Hos 6:4; 14:5; Mic 5:7; Hag 1:10; Zech 8:12). In modern times it has been found to be of special benefit to the grape harvest.

Springs

Today over seventy ancient sites in Palestine have the Arabic word *'ain* (spring) as part of their name. This is equivalent to *En-* in biblical place-names (En-gedi, En-gannim, En-rogel, etc). Since most of Palestine's rivers are seasonal (that is, they only flow during the rainy season), the main sources of flowing water which persisted throughout the summer were springs. Hence settlements grew up mostly around springs, and kept the same location over thousands of years.

Springs are abundant in limestone country such as Palestine. During the rainy season, water finds its way into underground cavities through fault-lines in the limestone, and then seeps out of these cavities as springs. A large enough supply of underground water ensures a constant supply from the spring, right through the dry season. Not all springs are perennial, however, and even those which are can fail in times of drought, since they depend ultimately on rainfall to replenish their underground sources. A spring may also become polluted and poisonous, as happened to the spring at Jericho in the days of Elisha. 2 Kings 2: 19–22 describes how Elisha purified its waters.

Streams

There are very few perennial streams or rivers in Palestine, and they are all fed by springs. The Jordan itself, for example, is fed by springs near the foot of Mount Hermon, whose melting snows increase their flow in spring, causing the river to rise (Josh 3: 15). The River Kishon is fed by the springs of Mount Carmel. Other perennial streams include a number of the Jordan's tributaries and four or five small streams which flow to the coast. The rest are seasonal.

Today a seasonal stream is commonly referred to by the Arabic term *wadi*. *Wadis* are simply dry river-beds during the summer months, but the onset of the rains transforms them into fast-flowing rivers, with grass and flowers springing up along their banks. The change can be dramatic, and there have been modern-day tragedies when children have been swept away and drowned by the sudden torrent.

There are several references to seasonal streams in the Old Testament. The Cherith by which Elijah lived in hiding was a *wadi* (1 Kings 17: 3–7), and Saul and his army waited in ambush in a dry river-bed during their campaign against the Amalekites (1 Sam 15: 5). Job compares his friends with a torrent-bed which fails to supply much-needed water in a time of heat (Job 6: 14–20). The danger associated with the sudden onset of a torrent is used as an image for the power of an enemy (Ps 124: 4; Jer 47: 2).

Wells

In some flat areas, especially in or near the beds of *wadis*, water remains in the ground long after the rainy season has ended. This ground water can be tapped by digging a well. Wells are a very old source of water. It has been noted that some settlements which date back to the late Neolithic period (8000–7000 BC) are located in areas where wells exist today, so perhaps wells were dug in those areas as much as 10,000 years ago. Wells were safer sources of drinking water than streams, which were also used for washing and had to be shared with animals. Wells provided water for animals too, but the water was drawn up in a jar and poured into troughs which the animals drank from (Gen 24:20; Exod 2:16), so there was no danger of contamination. When a well was not being used a large stone was placed over its mouth (Gen 29:8–10), probably to keep the water clean and to reduce evaporation.

The Arabic word for a well (*bîr*) is almost as common in place-names as the word for a spring. Its equivalent in biblical Hebrew is *beer*, as in Beersheba, Beer-lahai-roi, Beeroth, etc. This is because, like springs, some wells could provide water all year round, and so became the basis for permanent settlements. Permanent wells were usually very deep. At the Israelite (Iron Age) town of Beersheba, archaeologists have discovered a well with a depth of forty metres (140 feet) and a diameter of two metres (six feet). It had been dug around 1100 BC, and remained in use for hundreds of years. Although this well is sometimes called 'Abraham's well', there is really no possibility that it is the well Abraham dug at Beersheba (Gen 21:25–30), because Abraham lived about eight centuries before it was created. Furthermore, it seems unlikely that a well of such depth would have been dug by people who did not intend to settle there permanently. The Old Testament actually speaks of several wells dug by Abraham and his son Isaac, in the valley of Gerar and at Beersheba (Gen 26:17–25). These were probably shallow wells dug near the *wadis*, where ground water would have been nearer the surface. It is a practice of the Bedouin today to dig shallow wells, less than a metre (three feet) deep and about sixty centimetres (two feet) across, in the dry river beds. After a short time about 30 cms (1 foot) of water accumulates in the bottom. These shallow wells get silted up when the winter rains turn the *wadis* into torrents, and have to be freshly dug each summer.

Some wells were obviously shared by different communities, and could become a bone of contention, as in the case of Abraham and Isaac and the people of Abimelech (Gen 21: 25; 26: 19–20). Unnamed shepherds tried to drive the daughters of Reuel (or Jethro) away from the well where Moses rested in the land of Midian (Exod 2: 15–19). Such disputes simply reflect how precious water itself is in dry parts of the world. But wells were also natural meeting-places, as we see in Genesis 24: 10–27 and 29: 1–12.

Cisterns

A cistern was a means of collecting water during the rainy season and storing it for use in the dry summer months. Some types of cistern probably came into use in the Ancient Near East around 3000 BC. At the ancient site of Khirbet et-Tell (commonly thought to be Old Testament Ai), a large storage pool dates from about 2700–2500 BC. It was lined with stone slabs and sealed with clay to reduce seepage, and held up to 1700 cubic metres (over 60,500 cubic feet). Later cisterns were commonly underground chambers dug out of the limestone bedrock. Cisterns of this type were in use during the Middle Bronze Age (about 2000–1500 BC), though they cannot have been very effective until a type of lime plaster was developed (sometime between 1500 and 1200 BC) for waterproofing them. (In some areas, however, the limestone is naturally non-porous.) Joseph was thrown into a dry cistern by his brothers (Gen 37: 22–24). Since a typical underground cistern was pear-shaped (a bulbous chamber five to six metres [sixteen to nineteen feet] deep with an opening only about sixty centimetres [two feet] across at the surface), it would have been impossible to climb out of one without help. Over a thousand years later, Jeremiah was also imprisoned in a cistern, and although there was no water in it, it contained deep mud; he was eventually hauled out with ropes (Jer 38: 6–13).

The development of a lime plaster for waterproofing underground cisterns led to their much more widespread use from around 1200 BC, and this changed the pattern of human settlement in Palestine. Around 1200 BC new farming settlements appeared in the central hill country, away from springs and streams, and many of these owed their existence to waterproof plaster-lined cisterns. Plaster linings were not permanent, however; they could develop cracks and so have to be renewed. Jeremiah spoke of 'broken cisterns that can hold no water' as a picture of the false gods to which Judah had turned in his day; by contrast, the true God could be likened to a spring, a 'fountain of living waters' (Jer 2:13).

A cistern could either be large and communal or small and privately owned. Both types are referred to in the Old Testament. In 1 Samuel 19:22 Saul goes to 'the great cistern which is in Secu', while 2 Kings 18:31 and Proverbs 5:15 refer to the smaller, domestic cisterns. Archaeology has provided abundant examples of both types in many parts of Palestine. Beneath the houses of the Iron Age village at Khirbet et-Tell (see ch 3), storage systems of two or three connected cisterns were common. Two typical systems had capacities of about twenty-eight and twenty-three cubic metres.

Cisterns were used like wells, the water being drawn up in a vessel on a rope. However, whereas a well received its water from the surrounding earth or porous rock, a cistern had to be filled from the top. This was done by channelling rainwater from roofs, open courtyards and other areas where it collected during the rainy season. A waterproof cistern, with a stone cover to prevent evaporation, could have supplied water throughout the summer. However, if the autumn rains failed, cisterns were no substitute. Many were probably low by the end of summer, with a sediment of impurities at the bottom. Jeremiah's description of a drought (Jer 14:1–6) mentions how the nobles of Jerusalem

. . . send their servants for water;
they come to the cisterns,
they find no water,
they return with their vessels empty;
they are ashamed and confounded and cover their heads.

Town water supply systems

We saw in chapter 4 that the towns of Old Testament Palestine were usually built on hills, often on the tops of their own ruin-mounds. This gave them protection against attack, but made access to their springs (at the base of the mound) very difficult. It was not simply that the spring lay at some distance from the town, and made the carrying of water-jars an even greater chore than usual; it also lay outside the city walls, so that if the city was besieged its attackers could easily deprive its people of water. It was common practice for an invading army to cut off the water-supplies by stopping up the springs (eg 2 Kings 3:25) or taking them over for their own use if a long siege was planned (see 2 Chron 32:2–4). Without water, no city could hope to survive. Systems of shafts and tunnels were the answer to these problems.

Town water supply systems were ambitious engineering projects, sometimes involving techniques of construction which are still not properly understood. About a dozen of these systems have now been discovered by archaeologists at various sites in Palestine. Although they have certain features in common, their design varies a great deal from site to site.

Jerusalem

Two water systems can be seen at Jerusalem, both giving access to the Gihon spring, on the eastern side of the Old Testament town (1 Kings 1:33, etc). These were constructed at different times. The older of the two is known as Warren's Shaft, after Charles Warren who discovered it in 1867. Because it is generally believed to date from before David's conquest of the city (2 Sam 5:6–10), it is also known as the Jebusite Shaft. It consists of several elements. A horizontal tunnel (2)fifteen metres (fifty feet) long was cut through the rock to carry water westwards from the spring (1) to a chamber deep within the natural hill on which the city stood. From this reservoir-chamber another shaft (3) rose vertically for about the same distance. This met an almost horizontal tunnel (4) which in turn connected with a stepped tunnel (5) leading down from street-level inside the city (6). People going to draw water would descend this stepped tunnel (5) and walk along the almost horizontal passage (4), which passed beneath the city wall (7). They would then lower their jars on ropes down the vertical shaft to fill them from the reservoir below. There were two obvious advantages to this system: people did not have to walk all the way to the bottom of the hill and back again to get water, and the water-supply itself was

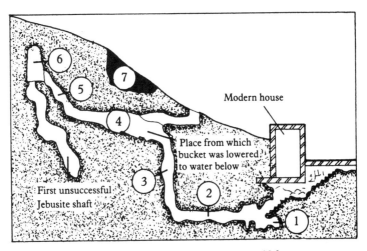

Place from which bucket was lowered to water below

First unsuccessful Jebusite shaft

Modern house

Section through the Jebusite water system: pre-10th century BC.

protected. However, it has been suggested that the arrangement was not completely foolproof, and that Joab, David's commander, gained access to the Jebusite city by getting into this system from outside the walls and somehow making the difficult climb up the vertical shaft (2 Sam 5: 6–9; 1 Chron 11: 4–9). On the other hand, the word *sinnor*, translated 'water shaft' in some English versions (eg RSV 2 Sam 5: 8), is actually of uncertain meaning, so this may not be the correct interpretation of the passage.

Later, towards the end of the eighth century BC, King Hezekiah replaced this system with a very different one. Archaeological finds suggest that Jerusalem was expanding in size in the reign of Hezekiah (see ch 4 on population figures), so perhaps the old Jebusite system was no longer efficient in serving the larger population. But the immediate reason for Hezekiah's project was to prepare Jerusalem for a siege by the Assyrian king Sennacherib, against whom Hezekiah rebelled (2 Kings 18: 7). The second book of Kings (20: 20) simply mentions that Hezekiah 'made the pool and the conduit and brought water into the city', but 2 Chronicles 32: 30 says he 'closed the upper outlet of the waters of Gihon and directed them down to the west side of the city of David', which may refer to the closing of the Jebusite system. Isaiah 22: 9–11 contains further references to this project, though the details are not clear; the verses mention that Hezekiah 'collected the waters of the lower pool', and 'made a reservoir between the two walls for the water of the old pool'. The context makes it very clear, however, that the project was part of Hezekiah's preparations to strengthen Jerusalem against a siege. The most vivid description of Hezekiah's undertaking is in the book of Ecclesiasticus (or Ben Sirach), written early in the second century BC. This mentions how the king 'fortified his city, and brought water into the midst of it; he tunnelled the sheer rock with iron and built pools for water' (48:17).

The tunnel which Hezekiah excavated through 'the sheer rock' was discovered in 1880. It follows a serpentine course, beginning from the old horizontal Jebusite shaft by the spring and making its way to the southwestern end of the 'city of David', where it still

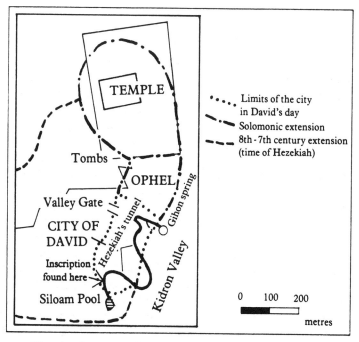

Plan showing course of Hezekiah's tunnel (or the Siloam tunnel).

feeds water into the Birket Silwan, the upper pool of Siloam. About five metres (sixteen feet) inside the tunnel from the pool, an inscription was found describing how the project was completed. The tunnel was cut by quarrymen working from each end, and the inscription describes the moment when the two gangs met:

> While there were yet three cubits to be cut through, [there was heard] the voice of a man calling to his fellow, for there was an overlap [?] in the rock on the right [and on the left]. And when the tunnel was driven through, the quarrymen hewed, each man toward his fellow, axe against axe. And the water flowed from the spring toward the reservoir for 1200 cubits, and the height of the rock above the heads of the quarrymen was 100 cubits. (NB, A cubit is about 44.5 cm [17.5 inches].)

A visitor to the tunnel today can still see the pick-marks of the quarrymen, and identify the meeting-point of the two gangs where the pick-strokes change direction.

The pool created by Hezekiah would have been a reservoir within the walls, from which people would have filled their water-jars.

Megiddo

The city of Megiddo had three water systems dating from different times. The earliest cannot be dated exactly, but it is almost certainly earlier than the tenth century BC. This was simply a small reservoir (2) cut out of the bedrock near the spring (1), and a set of steps (3) descending the lower slopes of the hill to this pool. When the city was fortified in the tenth century BC, probably by Solomon (see 1 Kings 9:15), this system was replaced by a gallery or passageway (7) which led from inside the city, through the city wall, to a set of steps (8) which descended to the entrance of the older reservoir (2). The gallery was about one metre (three feet) wide and two metres (six feet) high, and would originally have been roofed with wood and clay, as would the steps to the pool. This was still not completely satisfactory, however, as people still had to go outside the city for water, even though the gallery was covered. In the ninth century BC, probably in the reign of king Ahab, the third system was constructed. This was much more ambitious than either of the previous two. A huge vertical shaft (6) was cut through the debris of earlier towns, and through the bedrock beneath, to a depth of thirty-five metres (114 feet). A spiral of steps led to the bottom of the shaft, where a horizontal tunnel (5) sixty metres (200 feet) long provided access to the spring and its pool. The original entrance to the spring and pool was blocked by a great wall of stones (4), preventing any access to the water-supply from outside the city. This is an impressive engineering feat when one thinks of the labour involved in cutting the shaft and tunnel and clearing out the rubble. There was also great skill involved in correctly aligning the tunnel.

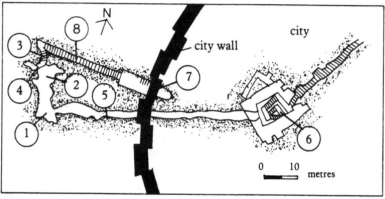

Plan of the Megiddo water systems.

Hazor

A similar system to the one just described was also found at Hazor, north of the Sea of Galilee, dating from about the same time. A vertical shaft (1) was sunk twenty-nine metres (ninety-five feet) through debris and bedrock, and from this ninety-three steps led twenty metres (sixty-five feet) down a sloping tunnel (2) to an underground pool (4). The pool was created by cutting out a chamber (3) below the level of the natural water-table, a total of thirty-eight metres (125 feet) below the street-level of ninth-century BC Hazor. This system lay completely within the city walls, and so was totally safe from attackers. It had not evolved from earlier systems like the one at Megiddo, and its construction shows no signs of false starts or experiments by its builders. It seems that they knew exactly what they were doing from the beginning. Because of this, it has been suggested that the designers and

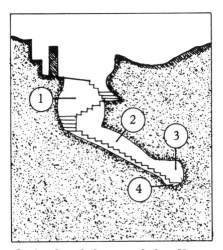

Section through the water shaft at Hazor.

builders of the Hazor system were putting into practice lessons already learned at some other site.

Gezer

Another site with a similar system is Gezer. Here the vertical shaft is only about ten metres (thirty-five feet) deep, and the sloping, stepped tunnel only fifteen metres (forty-eight feet) long, but the tunnel leads to a chamber at the level of the water-table, like the one at Hazor. Also as at Hazor, the whole system is within the city walls. There is a debate among archaeologists over the dating of this system. Some believe it dates from as early as the fourteenth century BC (ie in the Late Bronze Age), while others think it belongs to the ninth century BC like the ones at Hazor and Megiddo. The Gezer system was first excavated in 1902–1909, when archaeological techniques were still fairly crude, and crucial dating evidence was unfortunately lost in these early excavations. If the Gezer system was made as early as the fourteenth century BC, then it could have been the example on which the one at Hazor was based. On the other hand, if it dates from the ninth century BC, the Gezer and Hazor systems might both have been based on a discovery at yet another site.

Gibeon

While the type of system used at Gezer and Hazor may have been borrowed from as far away as Greece, it is also possible that it evolved in Palestine itself, at Gibeon. Gibeon, like Megiddo, had three water systems constructed at different times. The earliest was a large circular cistern (1), a pool cut into the bedrock some time before the tenth century BC. This was probably 'the pool of Gibeon' by which the champions from David's army fought the champions from Ishbosheth's army (2 Sam 2:12–17). This early cylindrical shaft was 11.3 metres (thirty-seven feet) in diameter and almost eleven metres (thirty-five feet) deep, and must have been used to store rainwater. At a later date, the cistern was emptied permanently and a further shaft (2) was created leading down from its floor to the chamber (3) at the water-table. However, this extension of the circular shaft was not the second stage of Gibeon's water system but the third. Before completing our description of it, we will give an account of the second.

The second system to be constructed at Gibeon probably dates from the tenth century BC. It consists of three elements: a stepped tunnel (4) forty-five metres (146 feet) long descends from inside the city to a water chamber (7) at the base of the hill and outside the walls. There was also an entrance (8) to this chamber from outside the city, as with the earliest system at Megiddo. The chamber received its water from a spring (5) deep under the hill. The water flowed from the spring to the chamber along a horizontal zigzagging tunnel (6) thirty-three metres (110 feet) long. This feeder

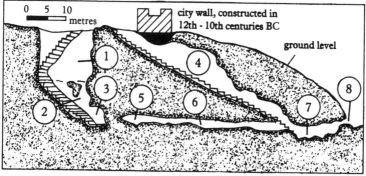

Section through the water systems at Gibeon.

tunnel seems to have been made by simply enlarging an existing fissure in the rock to increase the flow.

We now return to describing how the third system probably came to be built. Having excavated the feeder tunnel (6) to the spring (5), the Gibeonites must have realized that the spring actually lay very close to the earlier cistern (1), and that it could be reached directly by excavating a stepped shaft down from the floor of the cistern. Thus began a project to turn the cistern into an entrance-shaft to the spring. The Gibeonites excavated a narrow slanted tunnel (2) which continues down from the cistern floor for another thirteen metres (forty-five feet). However, although it slants in the direction of the spring, it never reaches it; instead, it leads to a chamber (3) cut at the level of the water-table. The most likely interpretation, it has been suggested, is that the workmen were heading for the spring when they *accidentally struck the water-table first*, and realized that they had access to yet *another* source of water! If the stepped tunnel is correctly dated to the tenth century BC, this third development, and the discovery of the water-table, would logically have happened at the beginning of the ninth century BC. It has therefore been suggested that this accidental discovery at Gibeon provided the basis for other water systems (as at Gezer and Hazor), in which a shaft and stepped tunnel lead directly to the water-table rather than to a spring outside the walls.

Other water systems
Beer-sheba also had a water system, in addition to the well described above. Stairs led down to the water-table of a wadi which runs past the foot of the mound. Other systems have been found at Ibleam, Tell es-Sa'idiyeh and Khirbet el-Khokh (biblical Etam). This last site has not yet been excavated, but we know it had a water system because the entrance to a stepped tunnel leading deep into the rock can be seen on the north side of the hill. Several more systems are doubtless awaiting discovery. At Lachish, a depression in the surface of the northeastern part of the *tell* may indicate the site of one.

The existence of these water-supply systems, requiring a great deal of ingenuity and manpower to create, is a powerful testimony to the importance of a reliable source of water in the Old Testament world.

CHAPTER SIX

Warfare

War was unfortunately a recurring experience in the Old Testament world. This was partly because of the Holy Land's location. We saw in chapter 2 how this affected Israel's history. Egyptian armies campaigned in Palestine and made it part of Egypt's empire, and also marched through it to clash with the Hittites and other enemies in the north. Later, Egypt, Assyria and Babylon fought over it and passed through it to fight each other. In addition, there were often internal wars between city-states, between established populations and new settlers (eg between the Canaanites and the Israelites, and later between the Israelites and the Philistines), and, of course, between the two kingdoms of Israel and Judah after the division of the monarchy. It is not really surprising that war provides the backdrop to so many of the Old Testament's stories.

Weapons and techniques of warfare were always changing, and a thorough study of warfare in the Old Testament world would have to look separately at different periods. The result would be a very large book on this one topic. All we can do here is to provide a very brief outline of the development of state warfare in Israel; then we will look at weapons and armour, and finally we will consider separately one aspect of warfare in Old Testament times: the besieging of a fortified city.

From tribal to state warfare

However far back the archaeological record takes us, it is impossible to trace a period when war, or at least the threat of it, was not present. The late Neolithic town at Jericho, one of the oldest cities in the world, had a moat, solid walls and defensive towers by about 7000 BC. Such defences obviously imply the likelihood of an attack. As we saw in chapter 4, the ruin-mounds (*tells*) of all ancient cities are a record of successive destructions and rebuildings, and it is a fair assumption that many destructions were the work of enemies.

Even before the rise of large standing armies belonging to nation-states, there was warfare between cities, between tribes, or between tribal groups and cities. Tribal warfare is first mentioned in the Old Testament in the time of Abraham. After a coalition of four Mesopotamian kings had invaded Canaan as far south as the Negev, taking Lot's family captive, Abraham led a group of 318 trained men in pursuit and rescued them (Gen 14).

When the Israelite tribes invaded Canaan under the leadership of Joshua, they did not have a professional army. It was the obligation of every able-bodied man to fight for the possession of the land. They were confronted by cities which were 'fortified and very large' (Num 13:28), 'great and fortified up to heaven' (Deut 1:28), and seemingly unconquerable. The tribes did not have the equipment or manpower to besiege such cities, and so Joshua resorted to very different tactics. He sent spies ahead to report on the lie of the land (eg Josh 2:1; 7:2; Judg 1:23–4), and sometimes relied on inside help from sympathetic Canaanites (Josh 2:2–21; Judg 1:24–5). He also used a variety of tricks to draw a city's defenders out into the open, where they could be ambushed (eg Josh 8:3–23; 10:9; 11:7). Only twice in the account of the conquest of Canaan do we read of the Israelites besieging cities, and these sieges lasted only two days in one case and one day in the other (Josh 10:31–2, 34–5). They were successful on these occasions because the armies of those cities had already been defeated on the battlefield (Josh 10:1–27), so they had few if any defenders. On the whole, Joshua's guerilla forces were most effective in the hill country; they were often unsuccessful in the plains, where the Canaanites were able to deploy chariots (Josh 17:16; Judg 1:19).

Throughout the period of the judges the tribes still had no regular army. Every man had an obligation to fight for his tribe in times of crisis, and neighbouring tribes were expected to help each other. Ultimately this was seen as an obligation to God himself. The Song of Deborah vividly portrays the rallying of the tribes for battle (Judg 5:14):

> From Ephraim they set out thither into the valley,
> following you, Benjamin, with your kinsmen;
> from Machir marched down the commanders,
> and from Zebulun those who bear the marshal's staff.

Bitter scorn was reserved for any who failed to respond (5:23):

> Curse Meroz, says the angel of the Lord,
> curse bitterly its inhabitants,
> because they came not to the help of the Lord,
> to the help of the Lord against the mighty.

Each tribe marched under its own standard or banner (Num 2:1–34). It has been suggested that these bore emblems based on traditional symbols for the various tribes (eg the imagery used in Gen 49:2–27).

The rise of a standing army in Israel came with the monarchy. We cannot be sure how far things changed under Saul, but the 3000 men which he chose (1 Sam 13:2) may have been a more permanent army than the militia raised by the tribal levy. Saul also collected a personal bodyguard of men whose strength and courage impressed him (1 Sam 14:52). More definite changes came with David, who appointed a permanent commander-in-chief over 'the king's army' (1 Chron 27:34). Another commander was in charge of troops of mercenaries from Cyprus and the Aegean, the Cherethites and Pelethites (2 Sam 20:23). There were various other commanding officers, 'the three' and 'the thirty' (2 Sam 23:8–39). As well as a standing army, David had a militia divided into twelve divisions, each serving for a month at a time (1 Chron 27:2–15). Each division was under commanders and officers (1 Chron 27:1). In times of national emergency, David could call upon all or part of this large militia to swell the regular army.

The military organization which developed under David probably remained the basic pattern throughout the time of the monarchy, though the army was constantly being 'modernized'. As we will see below, a large contingent of chariots was introduced by Solomon (1 Kings 10:26). In the eighth century BC, further changes were brought in by King Uzziah of Judah. The divisions of his militia totalled 307,500 trained men organized under 2600 'family leaders', to be called up by a secretary and an officer (2 Chron 26:11–13). This entire army was equipped with shields, scale armour, helmets, spears, bows and sling-stones (26:14). Uzziah also introduced the most up-to-date technology into Jerusalem, installing catapult-like machines which could shoot arrows and hurl stones (26:15).

The 'holy war'

Israel shared with other peoples of the Ancient Near East a basic conviction that the national god was involved in his people's battles, and that the god's honour was at stake in the outcome. God was 'the God of the armies of Israel' (1 Sam 17:45), and an early account of Israel's victories was called 'the Book of the Wars of the Lord' (Num 21:14). Battles were fought on God's behalf (eg Judg 5:23; 7:18), and God fought with and for his people (eg Josh 10:10–14; Judg 7:15; 2 Chron 20:17–23). However, for other nations of the period, a defeat meant that the enemy's god was more powerful than one's own; Israel's God was transcendent, and if Israel was defeated, it was because God had deliberately given her into the hands of her enemies (Judg 2:11–15). In his preaching before the fall of Jerusalem to the Babylonians, Jeremiah made it very clear that it was none other than God himself who had 'given all these lands into the hand of Nebuchadnezzar, the king of Babylon, my servant' (Jer 27:6, etc). In other words, Israel's concept of the 'holy war' was never meant to be crude nationalism. Israel could not automatically assume that God was on her side; if she turned from God's ways and standards, she herself became the enemy against whom God was prepared to fight (Isa 29:1–4; Jer 21:5–7).

Israel's rules for fighting a 'holy war' are set out in Deuteronomy 20, but there were special exceptions to these at the time of the conquest of Canaan. Notably, there was a severe application of 'the ban', the practice of giving a defeated people or city, along with its animals and goods, over to God. During the conquest this involved their almost wholesale destruction, as in the case of Jericho (Josh 6), so that the 'abominable practices' of the Canaanites would be removed from the land (Deut 20: 16–18). This was not, however, the standard practice. Deuteronomy 20: 10–15 stipulates that when an enemy city was conquered, its men were to be killed, and the women, children and livestock were to be treated as plunder. This meant making the women and children slaves. In practice, it seems that not even the men were all put to death in every case. When David conquered Rabbah and other cities of the Ammonites, he set their people 'to labour with saws and iron picks and iron axes, and made them toil at the brick kilns' (2 Sam 12: 31). This sounds like a project to clear woodland and build new agricultural settlements – unlikely tasks for women and children, even as prisoners-of-war.

Weapons and armour

Many types of weapon are so ancient that their origins lie in the obscurity of prehistory. Here we will concentrate on weapons known to us from the time of Abraham onwards.

The weapons of tribal warriors from the time of Abraham are depicted for us in paintings in the tombs of Egyptian provincial rulers who lived around 1900 BC. These rock-cut tombs at Beni Hasan, in Middle Egypt, are decorated with paintings around the walls, and military scenes figure prominently. Some show cities being besieged, while others show files of Semitic tribesmen armed with spears, bows and arrows, battle-axes and throwing-sticks (the Egyptian equivalent of the boomerang). The equipment of Abraham's fighting force (Gen 14: 14) was probably similar. All these weapons were of ancient origin.

The bow and arrow
Of the various long-range weapons developed in ancient times (eg javelin, sling, throwing-stick), the bow was the most powerful and effective. The most primitive type was a single arc of wood, but

more power was achieved by a double-convex shape, and two versions of this design were developed by 2500 BC, if not earlier. One type consisted of two antelope horns joined by a wooden centre-piece, while the other was all wooden. Later, perhaps around 1700–1600 BC, the even more powerful 'composite bow' appeared in the Ancient Near East. This consisted of laminated strips of wood, animal horn, tendons and glue. The composite bow required considerable strength and skill to use, and had a range of up to 365 metres (400 yards). The bow was not only used in war, but also for hunting animals (Gen 27:3), and this may have been its original purpose.

Arrows were made from a variety of materials. The shaft was commonly made of reed, but the head could be bone, flint, bronze or (after about 1000 BC) iron. Arrows were carried in a quiver which usually held thirty (or fifty if it was attached to a chariot instead of worn by an archer). The Old Testament contains a great many references to bows, arrows and quivers, reflecting their widespread use throughout the Old Testament period.

The sling

The sling was another very ancient weapon. Like the bow, it was not always a weapon of war. A shepherd would use one to protect his flock from wild beasts, as David did (1 Sam 17:34, 40). But David also used his sling to kill Goliath, the Philistine champion (1 Sam 17:49). Companies of slingers became part of the armies of Egypt, Assyria and Babylon, and also of the Israelite forces from David's time onwards (2 Kings 3:25; 1 Chron 12:2; 2 Chron 26:14). A sling consisted of a pocket of leather or cloth with a cord attached to each side. The pocket was loaded with a suitable stone and whirled above the head, holding the two cords in one hand. Releasing one of the cords flung the stone out at high speed. The stones used for ammunition were carefully rounded balls of flint, about six centimetres (two-and-a-half inches) in diameter, weighing about 250 grams. Sling-stones of this type turn up in excavations from almost all periods.

The battle-axe

A variety of weapons used in hand-to-hand combat throughout biblical times were of ancient origin. Several types of clubs and maces were used for striking the enemy, but more effective than these was the battle-axe. This weapon varied greatly in design. One ancient type, known from Egypt, had a semicircular head, like the axes used by Egyptian craftsmen, but by about 1750 BC a narrower axe-blade had been developed for use in warfare, more effective for penetrating shields and helmets. Battle-axes may be referred to in the Old Testament in Jeremiah 51:20 (see NEB; RSV 'hammer', NIV 'war club') and Ezekiel 9:2 (RSV 'weapon for slaughter', NIV 'deadly weapon').

The sword

The weapon most frequently mentioned in the Bible is the sword. This also had a long period of development. Examples from around 2500 BC are dagger-like: short and double-edged. By about 2000 BC a sickle-shaped sword or scimitar had developed, but blades were still fairly short. These were used like battle-axes for cutting or piercing, rather than as a thrusting weapon. It was between 1500 and 1200 BC that the straight, long-bladed sword came to be widely used. Blades were typically about sixty centimetres (two feet) long. The double-edged sword which Ehud made to assassinate Eglon, the king of Moab, was a cubit (ie about 44.5 cms [1.5 feet]) in length (Judg 3:16). From Assyrian reliefs and from the Bible (2 Sam 20:8) we learn that a sword was normally kept in a sheath suspended from a belt.

The spear

The spear of Old Testament times had a wooden shaft and a metal head (1 Sam 17:7). Spears were carried by troops of infantrymen (1 Chron 12:24, 34), and in the Egyptian army a lighter lance was also carried by charioteers. The Old Testament uses several Hebrew words for weapons of this type, probably indicating different lengths and weights (like our words 'spear', 'lance' and 'javelin'). For example, it has been suggested that the weapon mentioned in 2 Chronicles 23:10 was a short javelin for throwing, while a long spear is intended in Judges 5:8.

The chariot

The two centuries 1600–1400 BC saw rapid advances in the development of weapons and military organization in both Egypt and Syria-Palestine. Perhaps the greatest revolution during this period was the rise of chariotry.

Some writers have assumed that the Egyptians did not possess horses and chariots until these were brought into Egypt by the Hyksos around 1650 BC. On this view, the references to chariots and horsemen in the story of Joseph (Gen 41:43; 46:29; 47:17; 50:9) are unhistorical if, as the Bible's chronology requires, Joseph lived before the Hyksos ruled Egypt. However, the skeleton of a horse was found in the excavations of an Egyptian fortress at Buhen (now under the waters of Lake Nasser) from the period 1900–1700 BC. Furthermore, an inscription from the reign of the pharaoh Dudumose, who reigned around 1650 BC (just before the Hyksos assumed power), implies that a body of charioteers existed in his day. The references to chariots, horses and horsemen in the time of Joseph may therefore be treated as historical. On the other hand, their use does seem to have been limited at this time. It was not until about 1500 BC that the two-wheeled, horse-drawn chariot became a significant part of the Egyptian army, and began to play an important role in campaigns into Palestine and Syria.

By the time the Israelites entered Canaan under Joshua (see ch 2 for possible dates), the Canaanites were equipped with chariots. Indeed, it was because of these 'chariots of iron' (ie chariots with iron fittings) that the Israelites were unable to dislodge the Canaanites from the coastal plain and the Jezreel valley (Josh 17:11–18; Judg 1:19). Initial Israelite successes were in the central hill country, where the Canaanite chariots could not be used against them on the rough terrain.

The chariot's main contributions to warfare were speed and the element of surprise which this brought to an attack. The chariot itself was light, made of wood and leather, with only essential fittings made of bronze or iron. Each chariot usually carried its charioteer and a chariot-warrior, the latter armed with a bow and spear and carrying a shield. Sometimes, however, a third man carried the shield. The wheels usually had either four or six spokes, though heavier types (for carrying three men rather than two) with eight spokes to each wheel were used by the Hittites and the Assyrians. Each chariot was pulled by two horses. The various designs are well-known from Egyptian and Assyrian reliefs, and from actual examples found in Egyptian royal tombs. Chariots were driven into battle at full speed while the chariot-warriors fired their arrows into the enemy ranks. Scattering foot-soldiers stood little chance in such a situation.

The Israelites do not seem to have incorporated chariots into their fighting forces until the reigns of David and Solomon (10th century BC). When David captured chariot-horses from the king of Zobah, he kept enough for 100 chariots (2 Sam 8:4), and David's son Absalom equipped himself with a chariot and horses (2 Sam 15:1). Solomon considerably expanded this aspect of the Israelite army, creating a force of 1400 chariots which were stationed at Jerusalem and various 'chariot-cities' (1 Kings 9:19, 10:26). Solomon imported both horses and chariots from Egypt (1 Kings 10:28–9). His chariots seem to have had a crew of three, since the term šālîš, translated 'captain' by the RSV and NIV (eg 1 Kings 9:22) means literally 'third man'.

Israel evidently had a large chariot force in the days of Ahab. As we saw in chapter 2, when Shalmaneser III of Assyria clashed with a coalition of western kings at Qarqar in 853 BC, he recorded that 'Ahab the Israelite' had supplied 2000 chariots to the forces opposing him. Buildings thought to be stables have been excavated at Megiddo, dating from the ninth century BC, so Megiddo may have been a 'chariot city' in Ahab's reign.

A set of Assyrian reliefs depicting Sennacherib's siege of Lachish (in 701 BC) may depict Judean chariots of Hezekiah's day. They show three chariots being thrown down from the city wall onto the attackers below. Each has wheels with six spokes, and a yoke with harness-attachments for two horses. As we saw in chapter 4, it appears from Micah 1:13 that, in the late eighth century BC, Lachish was renowned as a garrison-city equipped with chariots. However, the chariots of Lachish may have been supplied by the Egyptians. In 2 Kings 18:24 the Assyrian field commander accuses Judah of relying 'on Egypt for chariots and for horsemen'. At this same time the prophet Isaiah spoke against those 'who trust in chariots because they are many' instead of relying on God to protect Jerusalem against the Assyrians (Isa 31:1).

Reviewing the role of these various weapons in the Israelite army during the monarchy, we can deduce from the Bible that it had contingents of archers (1 Chron 12:2; 2 Chron 26:15), slingers (2 Kings 3:25; 1 Chron 12:2; 2 Chron 26:14) and spearmen carrying shields (1 Chron 12:24, 34; 2 Chron 26:14). Exactly the same categories existed in the Assyrian infantry, and Assyrian reliefs show that soldiers in all three categories carried swords. And we have seen that there were also chariots in the Israelite armies, at least from the time of Solomon. It is difficult to deduce from the Old Testament whether a force of cavalry was ever important in Israel, but it is likely that at least some of the many references to 'horsemen' are to cavalry rather than charioteers.

Armour

Armour for defence was as important as weapons for attack, and various items are mentioned in the Bible. The use of shields dates back to at least 3000 BC. They were commonly made from thick hide covering a wooden frame, and they were oiled before use (Isa 21:5); hence when David laments the death of Saul, he speaks of Saul's shield, 'no longer rubbed with oil' (2 Sam 1:21, NIV). Sometimes shields were studded with metal for increased protection, but this had the disadvantage of adding to their weight. All-metal shields were probably for ceremonial use only (see 1 Kings 14:26–28). The Old Testament uses two Hebrew words for different sizes of shield. The larger type was that carried by spearmen, while archers were equipped with the smaller, lighter sort which could be pushed back over the shoulder out of the way (2 Chron 14:8). As we know from Egyptian and Assyrian reliefs, shields also varied in shape, some being round, others rectangular.

The head could be protected by a helmet, either of metal or leather. Greaves were sometimes worn to protect the legs (they were part of Goliath's armour, 1 Sam 17:6). By about 1500 BC scale armour was widely used for protecting other parts of the body. This consisted of small scales of bronze (sometimes iron in later periods) sewn onto a jacket of fabric or leather. It provided better protection than leather alone, without the enormous weight of plate armour. There could be over a thousand scales on a single coat of mail. Coats of mail must have been expensive items, and were probably limited to certain ranks and categories of soldier at most periods (eg charioteers and archers, who could not easily defend themselves with shields). However, in the eighth century King Uzziah provided the whole army of Judah with coats of mail, as well as helmets and shields (2 Chron 26:14). Coats of mail are depicted on many Assyrian reliefs of military campaigns, and the metal scales have often turned up in excavations.

Siege warfare

Siege warfare, by which fortified cities could be destroyed or forced to submit, is presumably as old as fortified cities. Like other military techniques, however, it evolved over the centuries (as also did methods of resisting it). It was the Assyrians who developed the ancient world's most effective techniques of siege warfare, and it was partly this which made the Assyrian armies such awesome opponents.

The besieging of a fortified city plays an important part in a number of significant Old Testament events: the fall of Samaria and the end of Israel in 722/21 BC (2 Kings 17), Sennacherib's invasion of Judah and his campaign against Jerusalem in 701 BC (2 Kings 18: 13–37; 2 Chron 32: 1–23), and the Babylonian attacks on Jerusalem in 598–97 and 589–87 BC, ending in the destruction of the city and the Babylonian Exile (2 Kings 24: 10–25: 21; 2 Chron 36: 9–21). These events form the background to a great many passages in the prophets. Some knowlede of siege warfare not only helps us to appreciate these events better, but in some cases aids our understanding of a biblical passage.

A siege was one of the most frightening things which could happen to a fortified city. Even if a good water-supply was ensured (see ch 5), food supplies inside the city could not last indefinitely, and there was no hope of getting more from outside. Not only was the city surrounded and watched at all times by the enemy troops, all crops growing outside the city were harvested by the invading army and kept for their own use. Starvation was therefore the fate of many during a long siege, and there are a number of references to this danger in the Old Testament (2 Kings 6: 24–29; 18: 27; 25: 2–3). Spring is referred to as 'the time when kings go forth to battle' (2 Sam 11: 1), and the availability of grain, which troops could seize for their own use, must have been a major reason for this. It meant that armies did not need to carry vast supplies with them on their long campaigns.

However, it was unusual for the attacking forces to do nothing while they waited for starvation to take its toll on the enemy. It was to their advantage to end the siege as quickly as possible, to conserve their own supplies. The Assyrians mastered a number of ways of penetrating fortified cities by direct assault, as we will see below.

Sennacherib's siege of Lachish

Our most detailed insights into siege warfare come from Sennacherib's siege of Lachish in 701 BC. 2 Chronicles 32: 9 says that Sennacherib 'was besieging Lachish with all his forces' when he sent messengers to Hezekiah to demand the surrender of Jerusalem (see also 2 Kings 18: 14), and 2 Kings 19: 8 mentions that at a later stage in the crisis Sennacherib had moved on from Lachish to fight against Libnah. These biblical references give us only a glimpse of what happened at Lachish. They do not even say explicitly that Lachish was conquered. However, our knowledge of events is greatly expanded by three other sources: Sennacherib's own account of his campaign, an extensive set of reliefs from his palace in Nineveh which celebrate his conquest of the city, and archaeological evidence from the site of Lachish itself.

As we saw in chapter 4, Lachish became the most important city in Judah next to Jerusalem itself, dominating key routes through the Shephelah. In the days of Hezekiah it was a heavily fortified garrison-city, with a huge palace-fort and a massive wall topped with battlements. Slightly lower down the slope of the mound this was encircled by an outer wall, also with battlements. Access to the city was through an outer and inner gate, the inner gate being the largest of its kind found in Palestine. Yet Lachish, along with over forty other Judean cities, fell to Sennacherib's troops. How was this achieved?

Sennacherib himself boasts in his account of the campaign: 'As to Hezekiah . . . I laid siege to forty-six of his strong cities, walled forts and to the countless small villages in their vicinity, and conquered them . . .'. He achieved these conquests, he says, 'by stamping down earth-ramps, and then by bringing up battering rams, by the assault of foot-soldiers, by breaches, tunnelling and sapper operations'. We know from his reliefs depicting the siege of Lachish, and from other Assyrian reliefs which show attacks on other cities, what these various operations involved. One of the

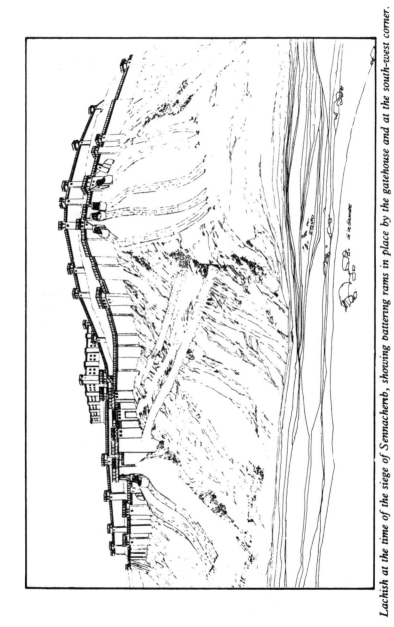

Lachish at the time of the siege of Sennacherib, showing battering rams in place by the gatehouse and at the south-west corner.

most comprehensive siege-scenes in Assyrian art dates from the reign of Ashurnasirpal II (883–859 BC), and it shows in detail five methods of attack taking place at the same time. On the left we see a storming party attempting to get over the city walls with the aid of scaling ladders. Next we are shown sappers demolishing the base of a wall with pikes; the loosened bricks can be seen falling to the ground. Then we see tunnelling operations going on beneath the city wall, either to penetrate the city or to weaken the wall. Finally, beyond the city wall to the right, a battering ram is in operation, and beyond that are archers firing volleys of arrows to provide covering fire.

Battering rams

The most interesting of these operations, and most relevant to archaeological finds at Lachish, is the use of battering rams. Sennacherib himself speaks of 'stamping down earth-ramps' and 'bringing up battering rams' in his attacks on Judean cities, and this has been very well illustrated by the Lachish excavations. In 1977 a huge mound of stones outside the southwest corner of the city was identified by the excavators as the Assyrian siege ramp erected in 701 BC. A siege ramp was a sloping embankment which enabled battering rams to be brought against the walls of a city. To create the one at Lachish, many thousands of tons of boulders had been heaped up to form the slope. The Assyrians had chosen the southwest corner because the city walls almost formed a right-angle there, so archers posted on the battlements could not concentrate their fire on the builders of the ramp so easily as from a straight line of wall.

The ramp was about seventy metres (227 feet) wide at the base, twenty-two to twenty-five metres (seventy to eighty feet) wide at the top and sixty metres (195 feet) long at the centre. In some sections there were layers of mud-brick or clay between the courses of stone, and the upper layer of stones was bonded together by a thick mortar. This was to provide a firm support for the weight of the battering rams. Sennacherib's Lachish reliefs show that wooden beams or logs were laid on top to prevent the wheels of the rams sinking into the surface or slipping. The use of wood in making siege ramps is referred to by Jeremiah, speaking of the impending siege of Jerusalem by the Babylonians (Jer 6:6): 'Cut

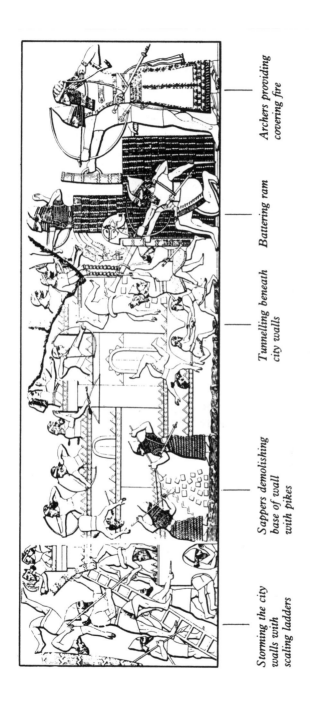

Storming the city walls with scaling ladders

Sappers demolishing base of wall with pikes

Tunnelling beneath city walls

Battering ram

Archers providing covering fire

Siege of a city, as depicted in reliefs of Ashurnasirpal II (883–859 BC) at Nimrud.

115

down the trees and build siege ramps against Jerusalem'. The manual for Israelite warfare in Deuteronomy 20 instructs the Israelites not to use fruit-trees for this purpose (Deut 20: 19–20). A wooden ramp surface at Lachish explains why Sennacherib's reliefs show the Judean defenders throwing firebrands down from the walls. They were trying to set fire to the wooden surface. One scene shows an Assyrian soldier, inside his battering-ram, pouring water on the ramp to prevent this happening.

The battering rams themselves were made of wood and leather, prefabricated in sections which were brought from Assyria and assembled outside the city walls. Those used against Lachish had four wheels and housed up to five operators. Inside, a heavy wooden shaft was suspended from the turret on ropes. The shaft was tipped with a metal point or an axe-like blade. It was swung against the mud-brick wall until it penetrated, and was then moved from side to side to loosen the bricks. Sennacherib's reliefs show a row of five battering-rams in use at the same time against the walls of Lachish, and the siege ramp discovered by archaeologists was certainly wide enough for that many.

The siege at Lachish took place in two stages. In the first stage, battering rams were brought against the outer wall. Evidence of fierce fighting has been excavated here, including burnt wood, ashes, scales of Assyrian armour, sling-stones and arrowheads. Twenty-seven arrowheads were found; one was embedded in the remains of the wall and several were bent, showing that they were aimed at the defenders on the wall from close range, using powerful bows.

Four links of an iron chain were also found. Chains were used as a defence against battering-rams, as we see from the relief of Ashurnasirpal II already described. Here the shaft of the battering-ram is shown caught in a chain, which is held by a man on top of the wall. He is evidently using the chain to pull the shaft upwards and out of position. To counteract this, two Assyrian soldiers are using hooks to pull the chain downwards, away from the shaft. In a long passage which speaks of the Babylonian assault on Jerusalem in 589–87 BC (Ezek 7: 2–27), Ezekiel refers to the making of chains for the city's defence:

Prepare chains, because the land is full of bloodshed and the city is full of violence. I will bring the most wicked of the nations to take possession of their houses . . . (7:23–24, NIV).

After Lachish's outer wall had been breached, the siege ramp was extended to get the battering-rams against the inner wall. This began the second stage of the siege, and must have struck terror into the hearts of the city's defenders. The fierceness of the conflict is reflected in the discovery of 157 arrowheads at the base of the inner wall (156 of iron, the other carved from bone). Heavy firing must have been needed to give the ramp-builders cover from attack.

The gradual extension of a siege ramp towards a city wall lies behind an important passage in Jeremiah 32. The setting here is the Babylonian assault on Jerusalem in 587–86 BC. God has commanded Jeremiah to buy a field – an action associated with planning for the future – to show that Jerusalem still has a future in God's purposes. After buying the field, Jeremiah prays: 'Behold, the siege mounds have come up to the city to take it . . .' (32:24). In other words, the ramps *have reached the walls* and the final assault is beginning. Jeremiah's gesture seems to have been futile. God replies that the city will indeed fall; his plan for the future lies *beyond* Jerusalem's destruction (32:26–44).

The use of counter-ramps
Returning to Lachish, archaeological evidence shows us the desperate measures taken by the defenders to strengthen the wall as the top of the siege ramp drew nearer. The people of Lachish dug up tons of soil and rubble inside the city to build a counter-ramp against the inner face of the wall at the southwestern corner. This lined the inside of the wall for a distance of 120 metres (about 390 feet), and in the centre was forty metres (130 feet) thick.

The people of Jerusalem may also have built counter-ramps inside their city as Sennacherib's army approached. Isaiah 22:10 speaks of how they 'broke down the houses [of Jerusalem] to fortify the wall'. A clearer reference to building a counter-ramp occurs in Jeremiah 33:4, which speaks of the events of 589–87 BC. There we read of 'the houses of this city [Jerusalem] and the houses of the kings of Judah which were torn down to make a defense against the siege mounds . . .'. A counter-ramp may also be referred to in Ezekiel 13: 4–5 and 22: 30 (RSV 'wall').

The fate of the conquered city

At Lachish all measures were eventually useless against the army of Sennacherib. Although it was 5.25 metres (17.5 feet) thick at the southwestern corner, the main wall was finally breached. Sennacherib's reliefs show some men of Lachish being cruelly tortured and impaled on stakes outside the conquered city, while the rest of the people are taken into captivity. Excavations show that Lachish was then set on fire. In some places burned bricks are piled two metres (six feet) high, covered with ash from collapsed roofs. The Assyrian soldiers must have gone through the city with torches, setting light to roof-beams, straw matting and anything else that would burn, until fire consumed the whole city.

In the 1930s the British excavators discovered tombs containing mass burials near the northwestern corner of the mound. Disarticulated skeletons of some 1500 people were found there, almost certainly victims of the catastrophe of 701 BC. These included women and children as well as men, and therefore represented civilians rather than troops killed in combat. Some of the bones were burnt and calcined. Exactly how these people died is uncertain, but their bones, along with the reliefs which show the survivors going into captivity, remind us that war brought tragedy, then as now, to ordinary people.

The fate of Lachish was the same fate which threatened Jerusalem itself in 701 BC. We can therefore appreciate the fear which gripped Hezekiah and his people (eg 2 Kings 19: 1–4). On that occasion the city was miraculously saved (2 Kings 19: 35–36), and Sennacherib was not able to boast of its conquest in his inscriptions or reliefs. However, little more than a century later, in 587 BC, Jerusalem's walls were breached by the battering-rams of Nebuchadnezzar. Thus ended a three-year siege. The cream of Jerusalem's population was taken captive to Babylon and all its buildings put to the torch (2 Kings 25: 1–10), fulfilling the warnings of Jeremiah and Ezekiel.

CHAPTER SEVEN

The Family

We discussed the size and structure of the family in chapter 3 when describing typical house designs. Here we will look at the family's role and function in Israelite society, the major events within a family's life, and the importance of family property.

The family in Israelite society

The three main units of Israelite society are distinguished for us in Joshua 7: 14, and are translated in English Bibles as (in descending order of size): tribe, family and household (RSV), or: tribe, clan and family (NIV). The unit below the tribe was therefore the clan (a preferable term to the RSV's 'family'). It is likely that this often corresponded to a whole town or village community. For a clan was a territorial unit as well as a group united by ties of blood. Thus in a list of clans in the tribe of Manasseh we find names which were also the names of towns (Num 26: 28–34). Clan unity was very important in Israelite society. Members of a clan were under a strong obligation to attend annual clan festivals (1 Sam 20: 27–29). Land was always inherited within the clan (Num 27: 11) and, as we shall see below, many laws existed to ensure that clan territory remained intact.

The smallest unit in Israelite society, apart from the individual, was that referred to as the 'household' (RSV) or 'family' (NIV). These English terms are alternative translations of the Hebrew word *bayit* (which is also the word for a house in the sense of a building). It is almost certain that this word refers in Joshua 7:14 (and very commonly elsewhere) to an extended or multiple family, that is, the occupants of a family compound. The extended family, or household, was therefore the basic unit of Israelite society.

As we saw in chapter 3, in a family of three generations, the head of the household would have been the grandfather. In the event of his death, the eldest son may have held that position, though it is also possible that households divided on such occasions, each married son becoming the head of a new household.

The head of the household was in a position of influence and responsibility. Within his family he exercised a kind of judicial authority. It was expected that a man would use this authority to ensure the responsible and godly conduct of his sons (1 Sam 2:22–36; 8:1–5). In Deuteronomy 21:18–21 we find a law that a persistently disobedient son should be stoned to death. This may seem excessively harsh, but it must be remembered that it applied to adult sons, not small children, and that the law assumes that discipline within the family has already been tried (vs 18–19). It is only when this internal authority fails that the matter becomes one of public justice.

The family head was also the *protector* of the whole household. No one suspected of an offence could be seized by his accusers without the authority of the head of his household (Judg 6:30–31; 2 Sam 14:7). Only a fool failed to protect his children from injustice (Job 5:4). The responsibility of a family head in this respect is only fully appreciated when we remember the scope of a household. The household was naturally responsible for the care of those of its members who were sick, elderly or disabled, and for its servants, but every Israelite also had an obligation to care for the poor in general (Lev 25:35; Deut 14:29; 15:7–11; 24:19–21; 26:12–13). Those who did not belong to households of their own, such as foreigners, widows and orphans, faced destitution (which could ultimately mean death from starvation) unless society made some provision for them. The Mosaic code therefore contained laws to ensure that people in those three categories were cared for (eg Deut 24:19–21; 26:12–13). Heads of households would have been responsible for putting such concerns into practice. Job is portrayed as the ideal benefactor, 'eyes to the blind, and feet to the lame . . . a father to the poor' (Job 29:15–16; see also verses 13–14). In short, the family was the institution which cared for the sick and the poor, and the family head was the protector of all those under his roof. It is not surprising that Israel saw God as its 'father' (Isa 64:8; Mal 1:6, etc).

Although family headship was generally a male role, it was not unknown for a widow to become the head of a household, even when she had an adult son. This is the situation depicted in 2 Samuel 14:4–11 (though the woman's story in this case is a fiction designed to appeal to David's conscience; even so, the situation must have been a realistic one). The wealthy woman of Shunem, who gave hospitality to Elisha (2 Kings 4:8–10), acts as the head of her household in 2 Kings 8:1–6, taking her family to Philistia for seven years and reclaiming the family estate on their return. She was probably a widow at that time, for her husband is described as elderly in 2 Kings 4:14 and he is not mentioned in the later story at all. If she is *not* a widow in 2 Kings 8, then the story illustrates the considerable authority and responsibility which some married women exercised within their households (see also Prov 31:16–29). Indeed, even while her husband is definitely alive this woman acts with independence and initiative (2 Kings 4:8–37).

Marriage

Israelite marriage was ideally monogamous, as is shown by Genesis 2:23–24, and by the many passages in the prophets which represent Israel as the sole wife of God. As we saw in chapter 3, however, polygamy (strictly polygyny, ie a man having more than one wife) was common in the age of the patriarchs, partly because they followed the custom of the time by which a man took a second wife if his first proved barren. This custom may have lingered on into the period of the judges, since Elkanah had two wives, one of whom was barren until she bore him Samuel (1 Sam 1:1–2; see also the legislation in Deut 21:15–17). On the other hand, many passages assume that, as a general rule, marriages were monogamous from the time of Moses onwards (Lev 18:18; Deut 28:54, 56; Prov 5:15–21). The kings were obvious exceptions to this (eg 1 Sam 25:43; 2 Sam 16:21; 1 Kings 11:3, etc), their marriages often being diplomatic in nature. However, in the Mosaic legislation even the king was forbidden to 'multiply wives for himself' (Deut 17:17).

Marriage within one's own wider family (ie the clan) seems to have been the ideal in early periods (Gen 11:29; 24:24; 29:10), and this may have continued through later times (though there is no law which requires it). On marrying, a woman left her own parents' household to live with her husband. Ideally the husband acquired a house of his own in the family compound, in which to start a family; in this sense he 'leaves his father and his mother and cleaves to his wife . . .' (Gen 2:24). Marriages were usually arranged by the two sets of parents or other close relatives of the prospective bride and groom, but this could be after the man had made his own choice of partner (eg Gen 34:4; Judg 14:1–10). It seems from the case of Rebekah (Gen 24:58) that the girl was sometimes asked whether she consented to the arrangement. We should not assume that arranged marriages were devoid of romantic love or sexual attraction. Indeed, the Song of Solomon celebrates the desires which exist between a bride and bridegroom at the time of their wedding, and Proverbs 5:19 urges that this attraction should remain part of married life.

A gift was given to the bride's family by the bridegroom or his family (Gen 34:12; 1 Sam 18:25, etc). This is sometimes referred to as the 'bride-price', but this is misleading; a wife was not sold and bought like property or a slave. Rather the 'marriage present' (RSV) was compensation for the loss of a valuable member of the family. Hence it sometimes took the form of service, such as the fourteen years of service which Jacob gave Laban for Rachel and Leah (Gen 29; Moses' work as a shepherd in Exod 3:1 should perhaps be seen in the same way). A dowry was also given to the bride by her father (Gen 29:24; Judg 1:15; 1 Kings 9:16).

The wedding itself was celebrated with a feast. It would seem from Genesis 29:27 that the festivities lasted for a week in the patriarchal period; in the intertestamental period they lasted two weeks, to judge from Tobit 8:19–20 (in the Apocrypha). There was evidently music and singing (Ps 78:63; Jer 7:34), and examples of 'marriage songs' are probably preserved for us in Psalm 45 and the Song of Solomon.

Deuteronomy 24:1–4 permits divorce, though the exact grounds envisaged there are not clear. These verses should not be read as a *command* to be applied whenever a man found his relationship with his wife difficult. They were intended simply to *permit* divorce in extreme circumstances, as Jesus made clear (Matt 19:8).

If a married man died childless, his brother was expected to take the widow as his own wife. The intention was that the brother would father children in the place of the dead man, and so the children of the marriage were to be counted as children of the *first* husband. This is known as a *levirate* marriage. (The term is derived from the Latin word *levir*, which means 'husband's brother' and hence has nothing to do with the Old Testament Levites.) The law concerning levirate marriage is found in Deuteronomy 25:5–10, which shows that a man could refuse to marry his brother's widow if he wished, though this was considered a serious betrayal of family loyalties. The sin of Onan in Genesis 38:8–10 was his refusal to father children on behalf of his deceased brother, even though he had married that brother's widow. He was in fact evading his family responsibility while appearing outwardly to fulfil it. His motive was that the children of the marriage would not be counted as his own (v 9). It is not clear whether a man was expected to marry his brother's widow if he was already married. Deuteronomy 25:5 refers specifically to brothers who live together, and so perhaps did not apply to those who had left the family compound and become heads or members of separate households.

The book of Ruth shows that the principle of the levirate marriage was applied in ways which went beyond the letter of the law in Deuteronomy 25:5–10. It is not her dead husband's brother, but an unnamed relative of Ruth's father-in-law, whose duty it is to marry her. Boaz, a more distant relative, was able to marry her because that kinsman did not wish to do so (Ruth 3:12–13; 4:1–12). Another extension of Deuteronomy 25:5–10 is that the kinsman was expected to marry Ruth, not her mother-in-law Naomi. This was presumably because Naomi was too old to have any more children (Ruth 1:11–12), and the fathering of children in place of the deceased was the main point of the arrangement.

Birth and circumcision, death and burial

The birth of children was greatly desired in Israelite families (Prov 17:6; Ps 127:3–5; 128:3), and for a woman to be barren was a cause of great sorrow and a source of reproach, as we see in the cases of Rachel (Gen 30:1) and Hannah (1 Sam 1:6–7). Sons were particularly desired because they perpetuated the family line. The birth of a child, and especially the birth of a son, was therefore a very joyful occasion.

The Old Testament gives us only scant information about how births took place. Mothers had the help of midwives (Gen 35:17; 38:28; Exod 1:15), and some kind of birthing stool was used (Exod 1:16). Exodus 1:19 implies that Israelite women had relatively easy deliveries, as is said to be the case with many Bedouin women today. On the other hand, the pains of childbirth were felt and feared (Gen 3:16), and are often used as a metaphor in the Old Testament (eg Ps 48:6; Isa 13:8; Jer 4:31; Hos 13:13 etc). The dangers of childbirth must have been well-known. As we noted in chapter 3, it has been suggested that up to thirty percent of women died in childbirth. (Rachel died while giving birth to Benjamin, Gen 35:18.)

A first-born son was of special significance, and had to be given to God (Exod 22:29). In the case of the firstborn animals from the Israelites' flocks and herds, this giving to God involved sacrifice (Exod 13:11–13), but God did not require human sacrifice. Instead, firstborn Israelites were 'redeemed' by the payment of five shekels of silver to the sanctuary (Exod 13:15; 34:20). This special significance was attached to the firstborn as a reminder of how God delivered his people from slavery by slaying the firstborn of Egypt (Exod 13:14–16).

All male children were circumcised when they were eight days old (Lev 12:3), the foreskin being cut away with a flint knife (Exod 4:25; Josh 5:2–3). This was done as a sign of the covenant which God had made with Abraham and his descendants (Gen 17:9–14). Some of Israel's neighbours also practised circumcision (see Jer 9:25), perhaps as a puberty rite, but only for Israel did it signify a covenant with God. Foreigners who wished to join the covenant people were also required to undergo circumcision (Gen 17:12–13; 34:13–17). Whereas the wound healed quickly in the case of small children, adults required several days of rest (Gen 34:25; Josh 5:8). Foreigners were only allowed to take part in the celebration of Passover when they had been circumcised (Exod 12:48), for this was a feast for the covenant community.

It may have been customary to hold a celebration when a child was weaned. Abraham celebrated this event in the life of Isaac (Gen 21:8). Weaning occurred much later than is usual in modern western society, as we see from the case of Samuel, who was obviously no longer a baby when he was weaned (1 Sam 1:22–24). 2 Maccabees 7:27 (in the Apocrypha) speaks of a child being weaned at the age of three. This refers to the second century BC, but the practice was most likely similar in earlier centuries.

In a world which lacked the benefits of modern medicine, the infant mortality rate was probably fairly high (one estimate puts it at forty percent). Incurable disease was common (eg Num 25:9; 1 Sam 5:6; 2 Sam 24:25; 2 Chron 21:18–19) and must have been the cause of many premature deaths. However, people who escaped such fatal illnesses seem to have lived to a ripe old age. Leaving aside the extraordinary ages listed for the period before the Flood (Gen 5), we have several ages well in excess of a hundred years recorded for the time between Abraham and Moses. (The reference to 120 years in Gen 6:3 is perhaps meant as the average for this period). After the time of Moses, however, ages at death seem to have been roughly what they are today in modern western society. Psalm 90:10 gives the human lifespan as seventy years, 'or eighty, if we have the strength' (NIV). The priest Eli lived to ninety-eight, though he had lost his sight by that age (1 Sam 4:15), and the chief priest Jehoiada rivalled the patriarchs by living to 130 (2 Chron 24:15). It was probably unusual for someone to live beyond 100 years in that period, but lifespans of seventy, eighty and even ninety years were not uncommon, as we learn from contemporary Egyptian and Babylonian texts. In Egypt the ideal lifespan was considered to be 110, but it seems unlikely that it was frequently achieved.

Death at an advanced age was accepted as the natural end of a full life. Nonetheless, it was a distressing occasion for the bereaved. Emotions were displayed much more openly than in modern western society, and mourning was a very public affair (Gen 37:34; 50:1; Job 1:20; 2:12, etc). Burial took place very soon after death, probably on the same day, as is still common in the East. There was probably a fixed period of mourning, though we do not know how long it lasted. The seventy days of mourning for Jacob (Gen 50:3) reflect Egyptian, not Israelite, practice.

The preparation of the dead for burial seems to have been very simple. The eyes were closed (Gen 46:4), and the body was buried fully clothed. This latter point is evident from archaeology, for pins and brooches (which are all that remain when clothing has decayed) are common in tombs of all periods. No kind of embalming was attempted, and no coffins were used. (Jacob and Joseph were exceptions, since they were both buried according to Egyptian customs; Gen 50:2, 26). Several different kinds of burials were carried out in Palestine during the Old Testament period, but the most widespread practice consisted of laying the body in a tomb cut out of the soft, limestone rock, or in a natural cave of suitable size. These burial places were used by families over long periods, the bones of earlier burials being moved aside to make room for later ones. Israelite tombs were evidently of this type. The Old Testament contains several references to people being buried in their ancestral tombs (Judg 8:32; 16:31; 2 Sam 2:32; 17:23; 19:37; 21:14), and the expressions 'to be gathered to one's people' and 'to sleep with one's fathers' (eg Gen 25:8; 35:29; Deut 31:16; 2 Sam 7:12) may have originated with this custom.

Tombs were usually located in recognized cemeteries on the fringes of the towns. Nomadic groups also had their burial plots to which they returned to bury their dead. Hence Abraham, Isaac, Rebekah, Jacob and Leah were all buried in the cave which Abraham had initially bought for the burial of Sarah (Gen 23:17–20; 25:9–10; 35:27–29; 49:29–32; 50:13).

Such tombs are often found to contain pottery vessels and lamps, perhaps items associated with the deceased in life. Ezekiel speaks of soldiers being buried 'with their weapons of war, whose swords were laid under their heads, and whose shields are upon their bones' (Ezek 32:27). We have no information from the Old Testament to tell us whether the Israelites shared the custom of placing such objects with their dead. If they did, it is doubtful whether the motive was a belief that they were needed in the afterlife. In the Old Testament period the Israelites thought of the afterlife as a very tenuous, shadowy existence in Sheol, the common grave of mankind. This was a place of darkness and inactivity, where God could not be praised and to which rich and poor, good and wicked, were all consigned (Job 3: 18–19; 10: 21–22; Ps 88: 5, 10–12; Isa 14: 9–11; 38: 18–19). Only rarely does the hope of something better find expression (eg Ps 49: 15; 73: 24–26) and explicit references to resurrection are found only in Isaiah 26: 19 and Daniel 12: 2. This particular doctrine did not become a mainstream belief in Judaism until the intertestamental period.

Family estates

When the Israelites entered Canaan, the land was divided up between the tribes. Within each tribe every clan had its own territory, and within each clan every household had its own plot of land sufficient to support it economically. A family's ownership of its estate was closely protected, for the family was dependent on it for its livelihood. Indeed, keeping the household and its land intact was the aim of a great many Old Testament laws, especially those concerning marriage, property and slavery. Not only the laws, but also some Old Testament stories, can only be appreciated fully when we realize how important was the preservation of the family on its ancestral land (eg Gen 38, Ruth, 2 Kings 4: 1–7; 8: 1–6; Neh 5, some of which will be commented on below).

The boundaries of a family's estate were marked by cairns of stones, and moving these 'landmarks' was strictly forbidden (Deut 19: 14; 27: 17; Prov 22: 28; 23: 10). This was because loss of the landmarks amounted to loss of a family's claim to its land. To move one's neighbour's landmarks was nothing less than theft of his land, which in turn meant depriving his family of its livelihood.

If a man became poor (eg through bad harvests) and got into debt, he might be forced to sell off some land in order to pay his creditor. However, it was important that the land should not be alienated from the family, so another member of the same clan was required to buy it back, if possible (Lev 25: 25). Failing that, the original owner was to buy it back himself as soon as his fortunes recovered (25: 26). In any event, a system of Jubilee years existed to prevent plots of land becoming permanently alienated from their families. In a Jubilee year (every fiftieth year) all land reverted to the families which had originally owned it (Lev 25: 13, 28). The Jubilee year was also a time for the cancellation of debts and the release of slaves (as described below). It was an economic measure to ensure that wealth (ie property) was not accumulated by a few at the expense of the rest. However, it would seem that the Jubilee regulations were often ignored, for the monarchy saw the rise of crown lands and large estates (1 Sam 8: 14; 25: 2; 1 Chron 27: 26–31), and the ideal of every man having his own plot of land evidently became just that – an ideal rather than a reality (Micah 4: 4; Zech 3: 10).

When a piece of land was redeemed by its original owner or a fellow-clansman, the purchase price was calculated in relation to the number of years to the next Jubilee (Lev 25: 15–16, 27). Ideally, land was never to be sold outside the clan in the first place. The story of Ruth involves the sale of land belonging to her mother-in-law Naomi, as well as Ruth's marriage to a relative of her dead husband. A near relative, who is not named in the story, had the first option on buying the land and was initially prepared to buy it. However, when Boaz linked the purchase of the property with the duty to marry Ruth, the man backed down (Ruth 4: 1–6). Perhaps he was not wealthy enough to buy the field and support Ruth and the family she might bear him. Boaz, a more distantly-related member of the clan (3: 12–13) but 'a man of wealth' (2: 1), was then able to act as next-of-kin, buying the land and marrying Ruth (4: 9–13).

In Jeremiah 32: 6–15 we have another example of land being bought and sold within the clan. Jeremiah is the cousin of Hanamel, the owner of the field in question, and therefore has 'the right of possession and redemption' (32: 8). Land presumably came on the open market only when a buyer could not be found within the clan at the right moment. As well as preserving clan territories intact and ensuring the survival and unity of families, the laws restricting the sale of land were a reminder that the land belonged ultimately to God (Lev 25: 23).

Debt may not have been the only reason behind the sale of property. It is quite likely that, as urban living developed, some people earned their entire livelihood as craftsmen or traders, and sold up their land to live and work in the cities. On the other hand, many who lived in the cities continued to own land (2 Sam 14: 28–

30; Prov 31: 16), employing others to farm it for them.

The buying and selling of land was done with an eye to detail which reflects the importance of land in Israel's social and economic structures. Jeremiah's purchase of a field from his cousin involved the signing of a deed of purchase before witnesses. There were two copies of the deed, setting out terms and conditions, one open and one sealed. These were placed 'in an earthenware vessel, that they may last a long time' (Jer 32:14). Given the right conditions, this could indeed preserve a document for 'a long time'; the Dead Sea Scrolls had survived in their jars for 2000 years before their discovery in 1947!

Sealing a document involved tying the scroll with cord and attaching a lump of clay or wax, on which an official seal was then pressed. Official seals varied in design, but those used in Palestine during the monarchy and the post-exilic period were oval, one to two centimetres in length, inscribed with the name and title of the owner and sometimes a simple design. They were usually made from semi-precious stones (jasper, rock-crystal, agate, etc). Over

A clay seal-impression belonging to an official of King Hezekiah of Judah. It bears the inscription: 'Belonging to Yehozerah ben Hilkiyahu, servant of Hezekiah.'

The seal of Shema, servant of Jeroboam.

200 Hebrew seals (or their impressions on clay) have now been found. One clay seal-impression actually bears the name and title 'Berechiah [a form of the biblical name Baruch], son of Neriah, the Scribe'. Since its style of writing dates it to the seventh or sixth centuries BC (the time of Jeremiah), there is little doubt that this was made with the seal of 'Baruch the scribe, the son of Neriah' (Jer 36:32), who was Jeremiah's attendant. As a scribe, Baruch was an official with the authority to transcribe and seal a legal document. Although the passage does not say so, it was therefore probably Baruch who set his seal to Jeremiah's deed of purchase.

The importance of a plot of land remaining in the same family underlies the story of Naboth's vineyard in 1 Kings 21. When Ahab asked Naboth for his vineyard, Naboth refused to part with it, even though the king offered him either its full price or an even better vineyard in exchange; 'The Lord forbid that I should give you the inheritance of my fathers' (21:3). Ahab's sullen acceptance of Naboth's decision stands in sharp contrast to the attitude of Jezebel, his queen. As the daughter of the king of Tyre, Jezebel shared the Canaanite concept of kingship, in which the king was the chief proprietor of the land and had absolute power over it. She had no patience with the distinctive Israelite view, in which *God* was the chief proprietor who had given the land to his people as an inheritance (Lev 20:24; 25:23) – a view to which even the king was subservient (1 Kings 21:3). She therefore set in motion a plot to confiscate Naboth's land illegally (1 Kings 21:8–16).

The family estate could be inherited by a man's daughters if he died without sons (Num 27:1–11). Indeed, the daughters of the deceased took precedence over his brothers (v 9). Women who inherited property were not allowed to marry outside their own clan, as this would have led to the break-up of clan territories (Num 36:5–12). Although the law makes no provision for a widow to inherit her husband's estate, it is clear that this did happen. Hence Naomi inherited the property of Elimelech (Ruth 4:3), and the wealthy woman of Shunem appears to have inherited her husband's estate in 2 Kings 8:1–6 (that is, assuming she was a widow by the time of that story, as suggested above).

As we have already noted, some land evidently became crown property under the early monarchy (1 Sam 8:14; 1 Chron 27:26–31). This could have happened in a variety of ways. It appears that land could be transferred to the crown if a family left Israelite territory and no fellow-clansman could purchase its estate. Thus in 2 Kings 8: 1–6, when the woman of Shunem takes her household to Philistia to avoid a famine in Israel, her estate becomes the king's property. However, when she returns seven years later she is able to claim it back again (v 6). The crown could apparently confiscate estates which had belonged to men executed for a crime (as in the case of Naboth, who was executed on a trumped-up charge). It is also likely that the laws governing the transfer of land were sometimes ignored, so that the king confiscated the lands of debtors.

CHAPTER EIGHT

Israel's Civil Institutions

By treating civil and religious institutions in separate chapters we make a distinction which an ancient Israelite would probably not have recognized. There was a religious dimension to *every* aspect of life. Hence many civil institutions, and laws which dealt with civil matters, had their basis in Israel's relationship with God. Provided we bear this in mind, however, it is convenient to divide Israel's institutions in this way.

Slavery and forced labour

Slavery was a feature of all societies of the Ancient Near East, including Israel. An Israelite could purchase a foreign slave from other foreigners (Lev 25:44–46), and sometimes foreign slaves entered Israelite society as prisoners of war (Deut 20:14; 21:10–14). Children born to slaves remained slaves themselves (Eccl 2:7; compare Jer 2:14). Foreign slaves were generally slaves for life, but they were protected by certain laws (Exod 21:20–21) and had the right to bring complaints against their owners (Job 31:13). They shared in Israel's festivals (Deut 16:11–14 – but in the case of the Passover, only if circumcised, Exod 12:44), including rest on the sabbath (Exod 20:10; 23:12).

But not all slaves in Israel were foreigners. For various reasons an Israelite could also become a slave to a fellow Israelite. Slavery for Israelites was to some degree a substitute for the modern system of imprisonment. A thief who could not pay the fine imposed on him had to serve a period of slavery (Exod 22: 3). Similarly a man who faced insolvency and could not pay off a debt became (along with his family) a slave to his creditor (Lev 25: 39–41). This had certain advantages over imprisonment, for it did not break up the family or cut the man off from society. The period of slavery for an Israelite was limited; it ended either at the next Jubilee year (Lev 25: 39–43), or after six years (Exod 21: 2; Deut 15: 12–18). On his release the man returned to his ancestral estate, and the creditor he had served was obliged to give him the wherewithal to begin normal life again (Lev 25: 41; Deut 15: 13–14).

An Israelite slave could also be freed by the action of a 'redeemer'; just as it was the task of the next-of-kin to buy back property in danger of being lost from the family (Lev 25: 25), a close relative could also buy a man out of his slavery (Lev 25: 47–53).

The regulations mentioned in the preceding paragraphs sought to control slavery and to protect the poor. Unfortunately the poor could still be exploited by the powerful and the unscrupulous. Amos attacks a situation in which 'the righteous' (ie those with right on their side in a legal process) were sold 'for silver, and the needy for a pair of shoes' (Amos 2: 6). This refers to a corrupt legal system in which the poor were sold into slavery for non-payment of minor debts. Their land was presumably confiscated by their creditors. Harsh (though not necessarily corrupt) creditors caused great hardship in the time of Nehemiah. Poor harvests, combined with the need to raise taxes for the Persian king, had forced many into poverty, and some creditors had demanded their lands and children in lieu of payment of debts (Neh 5: 3–5). Nehemiah was outraged when he heard of it, and forced the creditors to cancel all debts and return everything (5: 6–13). The poignant story in 2 Kings 4: 1–7 turns on a similar situation; a widow faced the loss of her children to her dead husband's creditor, who planned to take them into slavery.

The law expected a Hebrew slave to be well-treated (Lev 25: 43), and envisages a situation in which a slave and his family may wish to remain slaves for life rather than regain their freedom at the appointed time (Exod 21: 5–6; Deut 15: 16–17).

Foreign slaves were generally slaves for life, and were not released in a Jubilee year. There was a theological reason for treating foreign slaves differently from Israelites: God had redeemed Israel from slavery in Egypt to serve him, so it was inappropriate for Israelites to become lifetime slaves (except by choice), especially to foreigners (Lev 25: 42, 47–55). The Jubilee year was therefore more than an economic measure; it was a celebration of Israel's deliverance from bondage in Egypt to be God's own people (Lev 25: 38, 42, 55).

However, there were various ways in which a foreign slave *could* become free. A foreign girl captured in war might become the wife of her Israelite master, in which case she lost her slave status, and remained free even if she was subsequently divorced (Deut 21: 10–14). In 1 Chronicles 2: 34–35 we read of Sheshan, an Israelite who had no male children. He married one of his daughters to his Egyptian slave in order to perpetuate the family line, and the slave presumably became free at that point. Likewise, freedom was probably granted to Eliezer of Damascus, whom Abraham had appointed as his heir prior to the birth of Ishmael and Isaac (Gen 15: 2–3).

Forced labour was also a feature of Israelite society. It was a practice from at least the time of the early monarchy for the Israelites to subject conquered peoples to this kind of servitude. David used the conquered Ammonites for land-clearance and building projects (2 Sam 12: 31), and Solomon used forced labour for his extensive building programmes (1 Kings 9: 15–22). Both David and Solomon had an officer in charge of forced labour (Adoram under David [2 Sam 20: 24], Adoniram under Solomon [1 Kings 4: 6], Adoram again under Rehoboam [1 Kings 12: 18] – possibly the same person throughout). Although 1 Kings 9: 22 says Solomon did *not* use Israelites in his forced labour system, it seems clear from 1 Kings 11: 28 that he eventually did, and that this was one of the grievances which split the kingdom at Solomon's death (1 Kings 12: 4, 18).

We do not read of forced labour by name in the Old Testament after the time of Rehoboam, but it probably continued – and probably continued to include Israelites. Jeremiah had harsh words to say about king Jehoiakim, who built himself a palatial residence 'by unrighteousness, and his upper rooms by injustice; who makes his neighbour serve him for nothing, and does not give him his wages' (Jer 22: 13). This sounds suspiciously like forced labour. Indeed, a seal has been found from the time of Jeremiah which bears the name of an official called Pelaiah, and the title 'who is in charge of the forced labour'. In other words, Pelaiah held exactly the same office as Ado(ni)ram in the time of David and Solomon. Given the date of the seal (which is deduced from the style of writing employed) it is very possible that Pelaiah was the officer who served under Jehoiakim. In short, forced labour involving Israelites was probably an evil which continued (or recurred) throughout the time of the monarchy.

A seal dating from around 600 BC with an inscription which reads: 'Belonging to Pelaiah who is over [in charge of] the forced labour.'

Justice

Israel's civil and criminal laws were an integral part of the *tôrāh*, the body of 'statutes and ordinances' (Deut 4: 5, etc) which brought every area of life into a religious framework. (The Hebrew word *tôrāh* is often translated as 'law', though more accurately it means 'instruction'. It came to be applied to the first five books of the Old Testament, collectively equated with 'the law of Moses'.) The laws were therefore widely known, for the *tôrāh* was meant to be taught to every Israelite. It was to be read every seven years at public gatherings of men, women, children and resident aliens (Deut 31: 9–13). Nehemiah 8: 1–8 provides an example of such a public reading. Making the law widely known and understood was one of the responsibilities of the Levites (Neh 8: 7–9). They were sent out with various priests and officials to teach in all the towns (2 Chron 17:7–9). Furthermore, every head of a household was responsible for teaching the law to his children (Deut 6:6–9, 20–25; 11:18–20).

There is a theological basis to all the Old Testament laws. Since life for the Israelite was to be lived under God's authority, all offences were sin and to be treated with the utmost seriousness by the community. Furthermore, by living in accordance with the *tôrāh* Israel was to display something of God's character to the surrounding nations (Deut 4:5–8).

In terms of its practical outworkings, the Old Testament legal system treated most offences as wrongs against private citizens rather than against the state or the crown. It was the role of the injured party to bring the matter to court and seek redress. Courts consisted of the elders of a city and sessions were held publicly in the city gate (Deut 22:15; 25:7; Ruth 4:1–2, etc). The judicial powers of the elders were varied and far-reaching. They were to apprehend murderers (Deut 19:12), settle matrimonial disputes (22:15), deal with refusals to enter into levirate marriage (25:7–8), decide pleas of asylum from those guilty of manslaughter (Josh 20:4) and witness transactions such as the purchase of land (Ruth 4:4).

It seems clear that from time to time the legal processes lapsed or became corrupt and needed reform. We have already mentioned the corruption of the courts in Israel in the time of Amos (c 760 BC). About a century earlier Jehoshaphat had introduced reforms in the judicial system of Judah. He set up district courts in all the cities and a high court in Jerusalem (2 Chron 19:4–11). The latter was a central court of appeal to which difficult cases were brought from the district courts. Jehoshaphat may simply have been reviving an earlier system, for it seems that under David and Solomon the king himself presided over a court of appeal (2 Sam 14:4–17; 15:2; 1 Kings 3:16–28). Indeed, the promotion of justice was one of the king's primary duties: 'May he judge . . . with righteousness. . . . may he defend the cause of the poor of the people, give deliverance to the needy, and crush the oppressor!' (Ps 72:2–4). David's neglect of such duties allowed his son Absalom to stir up rebellion against him (2 Sam 14:1–6).

Guilt could not be established without the testimony of at least two witnesses (Deut 19:15). Bearing false witness in court was itself a grave offence. It was punished by whatever penalty would have been imposed on the one falsely accused (19: 16–21). Just as the initiative for prosecution rested with the plaintiff, it seems that the plaintiff was also responsible for enforcing the verdict in most cases. He may, however, have had the help of 'officers' (or 'officials'). These are sometimes mentioned alongside judges (Deut 16: 18; 1 Chron 23: 4) and perhaps they acted as bailiffs to ensure that judgement was correctly carried out. If so, they were the nearest thing to a police force in ancient Israel. In a case of murder, a relative of the victim (the 'avenger of blood') acted as executioner (Num 35: 16–21).

For a wide range of offences the punishment involved making restitution (eg Exod 22: 1–17; Lev 6: 1–5). Although a person could be kept in custody while awaiting sentence (Lev 24: 12), imprisonment is never prescribed in the Old Testament laws as a punishment. The nearest thing to it was the restriction imposed on someone guilty of manslaughter. Six cities were designated 'cities of refuge' in which anyone who had accidentally killed another could seek asylum (Num 35: 9–34; Deut 4: 41–43; 19: 1–13; Josh 20: 1–9). While there, the guilty party could not be killed by 'the avenger of blood', the relative of the deceased who otherwise had the right to put him to death. However, after the death of the current High Priest the guilty party was allowed to leave the 'city of refuge' and return to his own inheritance.

The death penalty applied in a number of cases: premeditated murder (Exod 21: 12–14), manstealing (Exod 21: 16), forbidden sexual acts (Lev 20: 10–13), disobedience to parental and civic authority (Deut 17: 12), idolatry (Lev 20: 2–3), sorcery (Exod 22: 18; Lev 20: 27), blasphemy (Lev 24: 11–22), false prophecy (Deut 13: 1–5) and breaking the sabbath (Num 15: 32–36). It is possible, however, that death was the *maximum* penalty for such offences, and not the penalty to be exacted automatically in every case. One reason for thinking this is that payment of compensation is specifically ruled out in the case of murder (Num 35: 31), implying that it *was* permissible for certain other offences, which deserved the death penalty only for their gravest forms. Perhaps the same implication is to be drawn from the phrase 'your eye shall not pity', used in relation to idolatry, murder and false witness (Deut 13: 8; 19: 13, 21); in other words, the penalty laid down in the law was to be applied to the letter in these cases, and compensation could not be accepted as a substitute. It is noteworthy that Nehemiah does not apply the death penalty for profaning the sabbath (Neh 13:15–22).

Although some of the Old Testament laws may seem severe by modern standards, we need to compare them with the laws of other peoples of the Ancient Near East to see them in perspective. In that context, the legal system of Israel stands out by setting a higher value on human life and family unity than on property. Hence offences against human life and the family carried more severe penalties than in other societies, while offences against most property required compensation rather than the death penalty. Offences such as blasphemy, idolatry and false prophecy carried the death penalty because of the paramount importance of Israel's covenant relationship with God. Such offences distorted or weakened that relationship and so were treated with the utmost gravity.

Administration

Israel's system of administration is rather difficult to reconstruct because the evidence (both from the Bible and from archaeology) is very incomplete. We can therefore give nothing like a full account of how the day to day affairs of the state were organized.

From the early days of the twelve tribes, even before their departure from Egypt, Israel had elders (Exod 3:16–18; 24:1). At that period the elders were probably the heads of families or clans. Later they were the leading citizens in charge of the affairs of the cities. As we have already seen, they also comprised the judiciary. It is not at all clear how they differed from judges, since the latter (as their name obviously suggests!) also had a judicial role (Exod 18:13–26; 2 Chron 19:4–7). Both terms probably embraced a range of functions which overlapped. The term 'judge' may also have had military overtones in some contexts, since it is used of those warrior-heroes from whom the book of Judges takes its name.

With the rise of the monarchy a centralized bureaucracy was imposed on the old tribal structures. David had a great many commanders, stewards and officials responsible for the organization of the military, running the crown lands and administering the state and its empire (2 Sam 8:15–18; 1 Chron 26:29–32; 27:2–28:1). As we saw in chapter 2, Solomon divided the land into thirteen districts (twelve in the north, with Judah apparently treated as a thirteenth) for taxation purposes. Each was under an official, and the twelve officials over the northern districts were each responsible for collecting taxes which went to support the royal household (1 Kings 4:7–19, 22–23). These were men of high rank, at least two of them being married to daughters of the king (4:11, 15). In addition Solomon had various other 'high officials' (4:1–6).

We are not told what became of this arrangement when the kingdom divided at Solomon's death, but Israel and Judah must both have retained some system for collecting revenue. In Israel Solomon's men may have been succeeded by those referred to as 'governors of the districts' (1 Kings 20:14–19); their duties included providing the king with a quota of armed men in times of emergency.

Archaeology provides us with occasional glimpses of the later taxation systems of Israel and Judah. The Samaria ostraca are important in this respect. Ostraca (singular 'ostracon') are sherds of pottery used as the ancient equivalent of scrap paper for jotting down notes. The Samaria ostraca are a collection of over sixty inscribed potsherds excavated at Samaria and dating from the eighth century BC. As an example, ostracon number one reads:

In the tenth year. To Shemariah from Poraim.
Jar of old wine.

Pega son of Elisha	2
Uzza son of Kabesh	1
Eliba	1
Baala son of Elisha	2
Jedaiah	1

The 'tenth year' is the date given in terms of the king's reign. Unfortunately the king in question is not named on any of the ostraca found so far. Shemariah is the name of the recipient of the commodity concerned, in this case jars of mature wine. Other ostraca record the delivery of jars of fine oil. The commodities named on the ostraca were probably taxes paid in kind, in which case Shemariah was a government official in charge of their collection. Poraim is the place (not otherwise known) from which he received the wine. In all, five officials are named on the ostraca, between them receiving disbursements from sixteen different places. After naming the commodity received, the inscription then lists the senders and the number of jars supplied by each one.

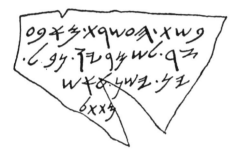

Ostraca from Samaria.

If this interpretation of the Samaria ostraca is the correct one (and others have been suggested), each recipient was a government official receiving taxes in kind from a particular region. So far as they can be identified, the sixteen places named on the ostraca lay in the hill country of Ephraim, which was one of Solomon's administrative districts (1 Kings 4: 8). It is therefore likely that the districts created by Solomon continued to exist after the division of the kingdom. Because Samaria itself lay in this district, it probably functioned as its administrative capital for taxation purposes, as well as being the capital of the whole kingdom. Other cities would have functioned as the administrative centres for other districts, and would have had their own officials equivalent to Shemariah and his colleagues.

The ostraca themselves may have been filed away as official receipts or, more probably, they were simply the rough notes from which a ledger was later compiled on a papyrus scroll. They are certainly evidence for a meticulously organized bureaucracy.

We also have evidence for the taxation system of *Judah* later in the same century. Dating from shortly before 700 BC (and therefore from the reign of Hezekiah) archaeologists have found literally hundreds of jar-handles bearing the impressions of royal seals. These have been excavated from various places, all within the boundaries of Judah. They bear a stylized design of Egyptian type (either a four-winged scarab-beetle or a double-winged sun-disk), a place name and the words 'to [or for] the king'. In all, four place names occur on the impressions: Hebron, Socoh, Ziph and an unknown *Mmst*. (However, the four Hebrew letters of this last name could be an abbreviation for the Hebrew word for 'government', in which case the place would be Jerusalem itself). These were probably four 'store-cities', that is, administrative centres around which the collection of taxes for Judah was centralized. The royal stamp itself would have been a sign that the jar was of the approved capacity for the payment of taxes. The jars probably contained wine and olive oil. We find 'fine oil' and 'new wine' listed in the Bible among the contents of Hezekiah's treasuries, which also housed silver, gold, spices, precious stones and grain (2 Kings 20:13; 2 Chron 32:27–28).

That taxes and tribute were commonly paid in the form of commodities is apparent from various biblical references (1 Kings 4:22–23, 27; 2 Kings 3:4, etc). Money in the form of coins did not come into use until about 650 BC (in Asia Minor), and coins are not mentioned in the Old Testament until the post-exilic period (Ezra 2:69; 8:27; Neh 7:70–71). The shekel used in earlier periods was not a coin but a measurement of weight (equivalent to about 11.5 grams or 0.4 oz.), and payment was commonly made in shekels of silver (sometimes gold). Hence when Abraham bought land from the people of Hebron he 'weighed out . . . four hundred shekels of silver, according to the weights current among the merchants' – that is, an agreed standard of weight (Gen 23:16). Similarly when Jeremiah bought his cousin's field he 'weighed the silver on the scales', a total of seventeen shekels (Jer 32: 9–10).

There are occasional references to taxes being collected in shekels of silver or gold. One of these (2 Kings 15: 19–20) concerns Menahem of Israel, who is said to have paid a tribute of 1000 talents to the king of Assyria, which he raised by levying a fifty-shekel tax on all the wealthy land-owners in his kingdom. (Since a talent was a weight equivalent to 3000 shekels, 60,000 men must have contributed to make up the total.) However, this may simply be a convenient way of quantifying taxes which were actually paid in kind. It seems from 2 Kings 7: 1 that a shekel was normally equivalent to either one seah (7.3 litres) of fine flour or two seahs of barley. Doubtless a wide range of other equivalents was in common use.

Archaeology has added to our knowledge of the titles borne by administrative officials, but unfortunately without clarifying the functions which went with them. Titles found on official seals include 'servant of the king', 'who is over the household' (ie the royal household; see 2 Kings 18: 18 where the same title occurs and is rendered 'palace administrator' in the NIV), 'retainer', 'scribe', and 'who is over the forced labour'. (See above on the last two.) Significantly, some official seals bear women's names, showing that women, too, held positions of responsibility in the administration. This should not surprise us overmuch, since even before the time of the monarchy a woman, Deborah, had held the office of judge (Judg 4–5).

Scribes probably had an important role as recorders and secretaries within the public administration and the royal household. The Hebrew word usually translated 'officer' or 'official' means literally 'writer', and so probably referred originally to a class of scribes which later became part of the 'civil service'. The 'king's officers' in 2 Chronicles 24: 11 were perhaps recorders of the temple revenues. In 2 Kings 18: 18 and 19: 2 we read of a chief scribe or secretary, who is mentioned alongside the palace administrator, the recorder and the leading priests as part of a group representing Hezekiah before the Assyrian commanders. He was therefore a man of high rank and may have been roughly equivalent to a modern 'Secretary of State'. The recorder (also mentioned in 2 Sam 8: 16; 1 Kings 4: 3) was probably responsible for keeping state records. Some scribes were responsible for military matters

(1 Chron 27:1, etc). It was only in the intertestamental period that scribes became associated primarily with the study of the law of Moses (the role which they have in the New Testament).

It would seem that major cities had a government official in charge of them, in addition to their elders (1 Kings 22:26; 2 Kings 10:5; 23:8). These were perhaps the officials responsible for taxes and military affairs in particular districts (the 'governors of the districts' referred to in 1 Kings 20:14–19). However, at least from the reign of Jehoshaphat (ninth century BC) Judah had military commanders and judges in every fortified city (2 Chron 17:19; 19:5). We should recall here the importance of the fortified cities in relation to the villages, already described in chapter 3. The cities provided military protection, judicial authority and general administrative oversight for their daughter-villages as well as for their own inhabitants. Jehoshaphat's officials would therefore have had responsibility for the surrounding villages in addition to the cities in which they resided.

Education and culture

In the Old Testament period the family was the context in which most children received their education. As we have already seen, each head of a household was responsible for teaching the *tôrāh* to his children, and this included instruction in a wide range of civil and religious matters. The great festivals, to be described in our final chapter, were also an opportunity to teach one's children the redeeming acts of God in Israel's history (Exod 13:8, 14–15).

'Wisdom'
It was also the responsibility of parents to teach their children 'wisdom', 'insight', 'understanding' and 'prudence' (Prov 1:2; 12:8; 23:4, 9, etc). These were the essential attributes for successful living, and so were intensely practical and not just theoretical. Their acquisition was grounded in religious belief: 'The fear of the Lord is the beginning of knowledge' (Prov 1:7).

It is clear that mothers were just as important as fathers in providing this kind of instruction (Prov 1:8; 6:20; 29:15; 31:26). Proverbs 31 consists of the sayings of Lemuel 'which his mother taught him' (31:1). It is partly because of the importance of the instruction received in the home that respect for both parents was commanded (Exod 20:12; Deut 5:16; Prov 23:22). Although biblical passages (Exod 13:8, 14; Deut 6:2, 20–21; Prov 1:8) refer only to *sons* being taught, it is obvious that daughters too were trained in the *tôrāh* and the art of wise living. Since mothers as well as fathers were responsible for teaching their children, it follows that they must have received the appropriate education themselves. There is no reason to believe (as is sometimes stated) that mothers only had the job of teaching homemaking crafts to their daughters. This is to underestimate the status of women in Israelite society.

Literacy

We cannot be certain how far education within the family involved the ability to read and write. It seems from Deuteronomy 6:9 and 11:20 that every head of a household was expected to write down parts of the law, and other references also imply that literacy was quite widespread, at least from the time of the judges, and not confined to those specially trained as scribes (Josh 8:32; Judg 8:14; 1 Sam 10:25; Isa 8:1; 10:19; 30:8). Archaeology supports this impression. From about 1200 BC it is common to find simple inscriptions, such as a person's name, on a wide range of items (arrowheads, pottery vessels etc), implying that either their owners or the craftsmen who made them were literate, and that they expected others to read what they had written.

Widespread literacy was made possible by the development of an alphabet around 1600 BC (perhaps in Phoenicia, but certainly in the Syria-Palestine region). Previously, writing systems had been immensely complex. For example, the cuneiform system developed in Mesopotamia from about 3100 BC had over 500 different signs. As long as scripts were so complex, writing was confined to élite groups of professional scribes. A simple alphabet of twenty-two signs put literacy within the grasp of many more people.

Whether Israel had formal schools and professional teachers is debated. Some see passages such as Proverbs 22:17–21 as evidence that she did. Others argue for them on the basis of analogy with Egypt and Mesopotamia, where schools are known to have been a very important part of the culture. It is also argued that the royal

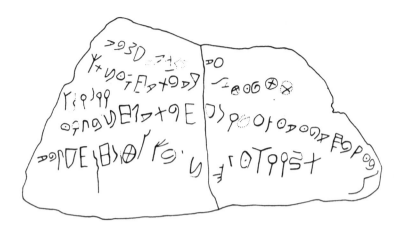

Proto-Canaanite alphabet on an ostracon from Izbet-Sartah, near Aphek.

administration could not have functioned without a class of officials specially trained in literacy, foreign languages and various other skills. This is certainly true, and we have seen that Israel did have its professional scribes. The question is whether their training took place in schools or some other context.

Archaeology may provide us with some evidence of scribal training. An ostracon found at a site near Aphek, dating from about 1200 BC, contains the twenty-two letters of the early alphabet along with copies of them done by a less sure hand. This appears to be a copying exercise. It has also been suggested that the 'Gezer calendar', described in chapter 1, was a young scribe's practice piece. However, even if such finds are evidence of training in literacy, we cannot be certain that they are evidence for the existence of schools. They could just as well be the products of writing exercises done in the home under the instruction of literate parents.

We therefore have to admit that we have no firm evidence for schools in Israel before the intertestamental period. However,

Israel surely had its political and military experts, and its mathematicians and engineers, and these must have received specialist training somehow. Perhaps particularly able children had their informal education supplemented by training from personal tutors. The seventy sons of Ahab had their 'guardians', also described as 'the great men of the city [Samaria] who were bringing them up' (2 Kings 10: 1, 6). As sons of the royal household they would have received training for a range of administrative duties.

Technical skills

We can deduce from archaeology that the Israelites had their trained architects and engineers, equipped with a good grasp of mathematics and other sciences. We noted evidence in chapter 4 for town planning, and this implies the training of specialists. The cities of Hazor, Megiddo and Gezer, rebuilt by Solomon, had gateways built to the same plan. This suggests a central planning office where plans were produced and kept for repeated use. The measurements of Solomon's temple and palace in Jerusalem, preserved in 1 Kings 6–7, imply the existence of plans which recorded the figures in detail. The accuracy with which square and rectangular structures (such as the governmental building at Lachish, described in ch 4) were laid out is evidence of a high degree of skill on the part of Israelite planners and architects. Finally, the complex water-systems described in chapter 5 are evidence of outstanding mathematical skills and engineering abilities. Specialists clearly existed in all these fields. It is often suggested that the Israelites relied on Phoenician skill in many areas of craftsmanship and design. This may have been the case, but there is no reason to think that they never made such skills their own.

Art

When we try to assess Israelite achievements in art, we have less to go on. The ivory plaques found at Samaria (mentioned in ch 4), and similar pieces from other sites, show a mixture of Phoenician, Egyptian and Assyrian influences and may not be of local manufacture. It has been suggested that they were the work of Phoenician craftsmen. On the other hand, it may simply be that the Israelites had the same artistic tastes as their neighbours, and that native craftsmen produced pieces indistinguishable from those made in Phoenicia or Assyria. Finely-carved Proto-Ionic capitals have been found at Megiddo and Samaria, and they give us a glimpse of the kind of architecture favoured for public buildings in the time of the monarchy. The Old Testament's descriptions of the style of decoration in Solomon's temple suggest a combination of Phoenician and Egyptian motifs (1 Kings 6–7). One thing is clear from those descriptions: the prohibitions contained in the second commandment (Exod 20: 4–5) were only understood to apply to the making of idols, and not to artistic endeavour in general. They certainly did not inhibit the decoration of the temple with numerous motifs borrowed from the natural and supernatural worlds (eg 1 Kings 6: 31–35; 7: 18–20, 29).

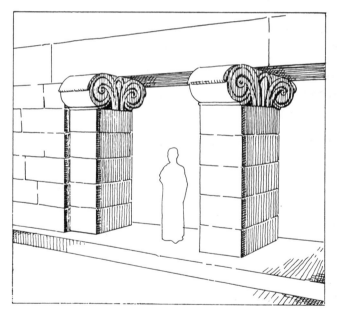

Reconstruction of entrance to the citadel at 9th-century BC Hazor (during the reign of Ahab), showing a pair of Proto-Ionic (or Proto-Aeolic) capitals and a lintel, discovered in excavation.

Music

Music was also an important part of Israelite culture. There were marriage songs (eg Ps 45 and the Song of Solomon), and, of course, the Psalms were written to be performed to music. It seems likely that every important ritual act had its musical accompaniment (see 1 Chron 15: 16–24). Music would have been part of Israelite folk-culture, too, and songs would have been sung while bringing in the harvest or treading the grapes.

Israelite culture must always have been open to foreign influences (such as we noted above when discussing the Samaria ivories) because of its location between other major cultures. The Israelite kingdoms traded with Egypt, Arabia, Phoenicia and Syria, and through those neighbours must have received influences from even further afield (1 Kings 9: 26–28; 10: 14–15, 28–29; Ezek 27: 17). While such contacts undoubtedly enriched Israelite culture (for instance, parts of Proverbs are closely related to Egyptian 'wisdom' texts), they also brought foreign religious influences into the life of Israel. In addition to the gods and goddesses of the local Canaanite culture, the Israelites were faced with the demands of the Phoenician Baal (Melqart) introduced by Jezebel, daughter of the king of Tyre and Sidon (1 Kings 16: 31–33; 18: 19). When Israel and Judah came under the Assyrian yoke, the door was opened to a host of unwelcome, foreign religious influences (2 Kings 16: 10–18; 21: 1–16). Egyptian practices can be detected in the abominations described in Ezekiel 8. The Israelites evidently found it hard not to adopt alien beliefs and forms of worship along with other aspects of foreign culture, and ultimately this was the undoing of both Israel and Judah.

CHAPTER NINE

Israel's Religious Institutions

Israel's religious institutions were not the same in all periods of Old Testament history. In the days of the patriarchs there was no priesthood, and individuals offered their own sacrifices (Gen 12:7; 13:18; 15:9–10). This did not stop immediately with the institution of the priesthood in the time of Moses (as we see from Judg 6:19–26; 13:19). Nor was there any immediate centralization of sacrifice and cultic worship at a single sanctuary (as enjoined by Deut 12). Anomalies such as the family shrine referred to in Judges 17 were probably commonplace.

It was not until the rise of the monarchy that it became practical to enforce centralization of the worship, and even then many of the kings failed to do so, as we will see below. Irregularities most naturally flourished in the northern kingdom after the division of the monarchy, because the northern tribes could no longer worship at Jerusalem and had no single sanctuary of their own. The two alternative shrines created by Jeroboam I at Bethel and Dan became centres of syncretism, the blending of foreign cults with the worship of the true God of Israel (1 Kings 12:26–33; 13:33–34; 14:15–16). Even in Jerusalem, however, the worship was not safe from pollution by pagan religions, and some of the kings sponsored foreign cults in the temple itself, earning Judah the wrath of the prophets (2 Kings 16:10–18; 21:1–9; Ezek 8:5–18; Zeph 1:4–6, etc). The trauma of the Exile purified the nation's belief and worship to some extent, but did not save it from occasional lapses in the post-exilic period (Mal 2:11; 3:3–5).

There is not space here to examine Israel's worship at each period of Old Testament history. We will therefore focus our attention on the First Temple period, the time from the building of the temple by Solomon in the tenth century BC to its destruction in 587 BC. We will, however, refer occasionally to earlier and later periods.

The Temple

From the time of Solomon the worship of God was focused at the temple in Jerusalem. The temple was the successor to the tabernacle, the portable tent-shrine which the Israelites carried with them as they travelled through the wilderness. In Egypt the concept of a portable pavilion dates back to before 2000 BC, so Israelites who had served the Egyptians as craftsmen would have been familiar with the techniques needed for its construction.

Steven's reconstruction of Solomon's Temple, showing the twin free-standing pillars (Jachin and Boaz), the vestibule porch and side storage chambers.

The form and size of the temple are described in 1 Kings 6–7 (compare 2 Chron 3–4), though the details are not always clear. Like the tabernacle, the temple was a rectangular, two-roomed holy place, but it was fronted by a portico which constituted a third room. The entrance to the portico had no doors, but was framed by two large, free-standing pillars known as Jachin and Boaz. (It has been suggested that these terms were abbreviations of inscriptions on the pillars, perhaps: 'He will establish [*jachin*] the throne of David for ever', and 'In the strength [*boaz*] of the Lord will the king rejoice'.) At the entrance to the holy place there was a pair of folding wooden doors decorated with palm trees, open flowers and cherubim. Cherubim are never described for us in the Old Testament, but they were evidently winged creatures (1 Kings 6:24). They probably resembled the winged lions with human faces which are a common feature of Syro-Phoenician and Mesopotamian art. Open flowers and palm trees were also common decorative motifs.

The holy place contained the incense altar, the table for showbread and ten lampstands, perhaps arranged in two rows of five along the sides of the room. Light also came from latticed windows set high in the walls. Along the exterior walls there were storerooms. At the far end stood the inner sanctuary, the 'most holy place' or 'holy of holies', separated from the holy place by doors and a veil. This room, without windows, housed the 'ark of the covenant', the wooden chest overlaid with gold which contained 'the testimony', the terms of Israel's covenant with God (Exod 25:16, 21; 40:20; 1 Kings 8:9). This was overarched by the wings of two large cherubim carved from olivewood and overlaid with gold. The space above the ark and between the cherubim was thought of in some sense as God's throne (Ps 80:1; 99:1; see also Exod 25:22, referring to the two golden cherubim which originally surmounted the ark itself, and which Solomon seems to have replaced with the ones described above).

The temple was not an impressive building in terms of its size. The holy place and the inner sanctuary together measured only about twenty-seven metres (ninety feet) long by nine metres (thirty feet) wide by thirteen metres (forty-five feet) high. It was not designed to hold huge gatherings of people, like a cathedral. It was simply God's dwelling place (though he was not thought of as being confined to it; see 1 Kings 8:27), and the place where the priests officiated. It was magnificent, however, in terms of its decoration. The doors, the altars, the interior wooden panels and the cherubim were all overlaid with gold (1 Kings 6:20–22; 28–35).

In the courtyard outside the portico stood a large bronze altar for burnt offerings, nine metres (thirty feet) square and 4.5 metres (fifteen feet) high; also a huge decorated bronze basin 4.5 metres (fifteen feet) in diameter, containing water for the priests to wash with.

The temple was intended to be the sole sanctuary for the worship of God. Prior to its construction there had been various lesser sanctuaries, some being places where the tabernacle and the ark occasionally resided. They included Shechem (Josh 8:30–35; 24:1–27; Judg 9:27), Shiloh (Judg 21:19; 1 Sam 1:3), Bethel (1 Sam 10:3) and Gilgal (1 Sam 11:14–15; 13:7–10), and numerous 'high places' where worship and sacrifice went on. After the building of the Jerusalem temple, worship at these became technically illegitimate. It is clear, however, from the Bible and from archaeology, that worship and sacrifice continued at such places. After the division of the kingdom the people of the northern tribes worshipped at the smaller sanctuaries, especially Bethel, and even in Judah the 'high places' continued to flourish in most periods (1 Kings 15:14). Archaeology has actually revealed evidence of local temples in Judah, for instance at Arad, Beersheba and perhaps Lachish. Worship at places distant from the capital was difficult to control, and such centres must have been especially prone to the deviant worship criticized by the prophets. In periods when the ordinary people of the towns and villages were not well taught, popular religion often degenerated into syncretism.

The temple built by Solomon was destroyed, along with the rest of Jerusalem, by the Babylonians in 587 BC (2 Kings 24:9–17), but a new temple was built after the exile. It was built on the Solomonic foundations (Ezra 4:12; 5:16), and so must have had the same dimensions, but did not match it in magnificence. The second temple contained no ark in its inner sanctuary, for that had been lost when the first temple was destroyed, and it was never replaced (see Jer 3:16).

Sacrifices, Priests and Levites

It is perhaps impossible for us to appreciate the significance which sacrifices had in Old Testament Israel and other ancient societies. To our way of thinking the rituals are too complex and bloody to have any appeal. They are perhaps the hardest aspect of Israelite society for us to understand. For Old Testament men and women, however, the sacrificial system embodied powerful concepts to do with the wholeness of society and its relationship with God.

A great variety of sacrifices were carried on at the temple (and earlier in the tabernacle and at the lesser sanctuaries), and they cannot all be discussed here. (Most are described in Lev 1–7.) There were, however, three basic categories. Some were intended as a gift to God, some served to unite the community, and some effected reconciliation between man and God. But the distinction should not be pressed too far, because all three aspects were present to some degree in all the sacrifices.

The sacrifice which best exemplifies the unconditional gift is *the burnt offering* (Lev 1: 1–17; 6: 8–13). The Hebrew term for this means literally 'that which ascends', and the sacrifice was probably thought of as 'going up in smoke' to God. The offerer received back no part of the animal (usually an ox, sheep or goat) for himself. An element of atonement was present when the offerer placed his hand on the animal's head (1: 4), perhaps to indicate that it was sacrificed as his representative. The animal had to be without blemish and male – that is, the costliest available.

While any worshipper could bring an occasional sacrifice to the priests for a burnt offering (1: 3–17), two lambs were offered daily in this way in the tabernacle and the temple, one in the morning and one in the evening (Exod 29: 38–42). Burnt offerings were also a feature of the three annual pilgrim festivals, which will be described below.

The peace offerings (Lev 3) were an occasion for community fellowship. (Indeed, the NIV calls these 'fellowship offerings' in preference to the traditional name.) The animal could be male or female, ox, lamb or goat, and the procedure partly resembled that for the burnt offerings. However, only parts of the animal (chiefly the fat) were burnt. Two portions of the animal were given to the priest, and the rest was consumed at a feast by the worshipper, his household and friends. Hence the peace offering was a time of festivity and rejoicing (1 Sam 11:15; 2 Sam 6:18–19). It expressed fellowship with God and fellowship between God's people.

The reconciling or expiatory nature of a sacrifice was to the fore in *the sin-offerings and guilt-offerings* (Lev 4:1–6:7). The difference between the two is by no means clear. The important feature of both was the use of the animal's blood. In burnt offerings and peace offerings the blood was cast against the altar by the priests. However, to atone for the sin of the high priest or the whole people the blood of the sin- and guilt-offerings was used in three different ways. Some was sprinkled before the veil which divided the inner sanctuary from the holy place, some was put on the 'horns' (the raised corners) of the incense altar, and the rest was poured at the base of the altar of burnt offerings. The meaning of this ritual was probably that access to both the innermost and outermost things of God, prevented by sin, was restored by the shed blood. In the case of a sacrifice for an individual the blood was applied to the altar of burnt offerings; symbolically this was the usual meeting place with God for the individual, so it was here that the relationship had to be restored. The unique role of blood in making atonement for sin is explained in Leviticus 17:11: 'For the life of the flesh is in the blood . . . It is the blood that makes atonement, by reason of the life'.

Sin-offerings formed part of the annual Day of Atonement, described in Leviticus 16. This fell on the tenth day of the seventh month and was an occasion when the high priest atoned for the sins of the whole people. He first offered a bull for himself and the priesthood, then took some of its blood into the inner sanctuary, where he sprinkled it on the covering lid ('mercy seat') of the ark. One of two goats was then sacrificed and its blood used in the same way. This was the *only* day each year when the high priest entered the inner sanctuary. The second goat then had a confession of sin recited over it before being led into the wilderness and released. This was the 'scapegoat' whose symbolic role was to 'bear all their iniquities upon him to a solitary land' (16:22).

The sacrifices emphasized the holiness of God and the gulf which existed between him and the worshipper. Only the priests could approach the altar of burnt offering, and only the high priest could enter the inner sanctuary, and on only one day of the year.

Nevertheless many people took the system for granted and assumed the automatic efficacy of the sacrifices. The prophets had to give strong reminders that sacrifice was meaningless unless worshippers had the right attitude to God and lived by the laws of the covenant (Isa 1: 10–17; Jer 7: 21–26; Amos 5: 21–24; Micah 6: 6–8).

In addition to offering the sacrifices, the priests were teachers of the law of Moses (Lev 10: 11; Mal 2: 7). When the ordinary people went astray from true worship, the priests bore a large share of the responsibility, because it reflected their failure to teach the *tôrāh* faithfully (Hos 4: 4–10; Mal 2: 7–9). Since they were experts in the *tôrāh*, they also acted as advisory councils to the judges in difficult cases (Deut 17: 8–9).

In these duties they were aided by the Levites. All priests were descendants of Aaron and so were members of the tribe of Levi (Exod 6: 16–20), but not all Levites were priests. The rest formed a body of assistants to the priests, helping them slaughter and skin animals for sacrifice, working as gatekeepers, musicians and singers in the temple, and, in their role as judges and scribes, sharing in the task of teaching and upholding the law (Num 8: 14–19; 1 Chron 23: 24–32; 2 Chron 5: 12–13; 17: 7–9; 19: 8). The Levites received no tribal territory of their own. Instead there were forty-eight 'Levitical cities', each with its own pasture lands, scattered through the territories of the other tribes (Num 18: 20; 35: 1–8). The Levites were supported by the tithes of the people, in which the priests also shared (Num 18: 21–32).

The festivals

Ancient Israel had two calendars. In one, the year began and ended in spring. Hence the month Abib (mid-March to mid-April, called Nisan in the post-exilic period), in which Passover falls, is described as 'the first month of the year' (Exod 12: 2). In the other, the year began and ended in the autumn with the Feast of Ingathering (Exod 23: 16; 34: 22), which celebrated the fruit harvest. The 'Gezer calendar' discussed in chapter 1 depends on this reckoning, beginning its account of the year in the autumn. Sometimes, to the potential confusion of the modern reader, both calendars are reflected in the same Old Testament passage. In Lev 25: 8–10 we find the year of Jubilee beginning in 'the seventh month' (ie mid-September to mid-October, called Ethanim in 1 Kings 8: 2 but known as Tishri in the post-exilic period). Beginning the Jubilee year at that point obviously reflects an *autumn* new year, while the reference to 'the seventh month' depends on the *spring* new year! (Today the Jewish new year is celebrated in the autumn.) Perhaps one system was the civil calendar and the other was the religious and agricultural calendar. When reading the Old Testament references to the festivals, we should note that these events were tied to the agricultural year (beginning in autumn), although their dates are often given in terms of the spring new year.

Several festivals punctuated life for the Israelites. There was the weekly *sabbath* rest (Exod 20: 11; 23: 12; Deut 5: 15) and a monthly *festival of the 'new moon'* (Num 10: 10; 28: 11–15). The seventh month (the turn of the year in the agricultural calendar) began with the *Feast of Trumpets* (Num 29: 1–6), followed on the tenth day by the *Day of Atonement* (29: 7–11; Lev 16: 29–34). This was followed five days later by the *Feast of Booths*, one of the three national pilgrimages to be described below. All these were marked by special sacrifices except for the sabbath, on which the daily burnt offerings in the temple were doubled.

The high points of the year were the three great pilgrim festivals (Exod 23: 14–17; Deut 16: 16–17). For these it was expected that every male would journey to the central sanctuary (ie Jerusalem after the building of the temple). Whether this applied only to *adult* males is not clear, but in any case it was probably understood as the *minimum* expectation, so that entire households made the journey together, as they certainly did in New Testament times (see Luke 2: 41–44). This is actually encouraged by Deuteronomy 16: 11, 14. These three festivals were as follows:

Passover and the Feast of Unleavened Bread (Exod 12: 1–20; Lev 23: 4–14; Num 28: 16–25; Deut 16: 1–8). These brought together the pastoral and agricultural aspects of Israel's life in a celebration of the deliverance from Egypt. The festival began on the fourteenth day of the spring month Abib and lasted for a week.

The Feast of Weeks (Lev 23: 15–22; Num 28: 26–31; Deut 16: 9–12). This was celebrated fifty days after the offering of the barley-sheaf during the Feast of Unleavened Bread (Lev 23: 10), and for this reason was later known as Pentecost (Acts 2:1), from the Greek for 'fiftieth'. It was marked by offerings of cereals and loaves of bread as well as animal sacrifices, and was a thanksgiving for the grain harvest. (Exod 23:16 calls it the Feast of Harvest.) While celebrating God's bounty, Israel also had to remember the needs of the poor (Lev 23:22).

The Feast of Booths or Tabernacles (Lev 23:33–43; Num 29:12–38; Deut 16:13–15). This was also called the Feast of Ingathering (Exod 23:16). It was an autumn festival to celebrate the end of the fruit harvest, and began five days after the Day of Atonement. The people spent the week living in shelters made from branches (the 'booths' or 'tabernacles' from which the event takes its name). This reflects a common practice during harvest time, when people camped out in the fields. However, as well as celebrating the fruit harvest this was a reminder that Israel had once lived in tents in the wilderness (Lev 23:43). The aim was perhaps to encourage a deeper appreciation of the blessings of permanent land and homes as well as the blessing of the harvest (Deut 6:10–12). The special sacrifices to be offered at all three of the great festivals are listed in Numbers 29, and the quantity prescribed for the Feast of Booths (vs 12–38) marks it out as the most important festival of the year.

Although it is only stipulated that every *male* should 'appear before the Lord' at the great pilgrim festivals, they were clearly intended to involve everyone, including children, servants, widows, orphans and even resident aliens (Deut 16:11, 14). The festivals were occasions for rest from everyday work, combining 'solemn assembly' with times to 'rejoice before the Lord your God' (Lev 23:36, 40). Because everyone was involved and every family was represented at the central sanctuary, they strengthened the Israelite's sense of belonging to the people of God. They also combined celebration of God's bounty at the harvest times with celebration of his mighty acts in Israel's history. In other words, they brought together an awareness of God's constant provision and a sense of history, purpose and meaning, reminding the Israelite that *every* area of life was to be lived in gratitude and service under God's sovereignty.

Time charts for Mesopotamia and Egypt

MESOPOTAMIA
3rd–2nd millennia BC (main periods)
3100–2700 Uruk IV–Early Dynastic I
Periods
2600–2370 3rd Early Dynastic Period
2370–2228 Old Akkadian (Agade) Period
2113–1991 3rd Dynasty of Ur
1991–1786 Isin-Larsa Dynasties
1894–1595 Old Babylonian Period
(1st Dynasty of Babylon)
1605–1150 Kassite Period

1st millennium BC
ASSYRIAN EMPIRE
883–859 Ashurnasirpal II
858–824 Shalmaneser III
853 *Battle of Qarqar*
823–811 Shamshi-Adad
810–783 Adad-nirari III
782–773 Shalmaneser IV
772–756 Ashurdan
755–745 Ashurnirari V
744–727 Tiglath-pileser III
726–722 Shalmaneser V
721–705 Sargon II
704–681 Sennacherib
680–669 Esarhaddon
668–630 Ashurbanipal
629–627 Ashuretililani
626–612 Sinsharishkun
612 *Fall of Nineveh*
612–609 Ashuruballit
609 *Fall of Haran*

BABYLONIAN EMPIRE
626–605 Nabopolassar
605–562 Nebuchadrezzar II
562–560 Amēl-Marduk (Evil-merodach)
562 *Captive Jehoiachin favoured by
Amēl-Marduk*
560–556 Neriglissar
556 Labashi-Marduk
556–539 Nabonidus, Belshazzar
539 *Fall of Babylon*

PERSIAN EMPIRE
539–530 Cyrus
530–522 Cambyses
522–486 Darius I
486–465/4 Xerxes I (Ahasuerus)
464–423 Artaxerxes I
423–404 Darius II Nothus
404–359 Artaxerxes II Mnemon
359/8–338/7 Artaxerxes III Ochus
338/7–336/5 Arses

336/5–331 Darius III Codomanus
331–323 Alexander of Macedon

EGYPT
3rd millennium BC
*c.*3100–2575 Archaic Period
(Protodynastic): Dynasties 1–2
*c.*2575–2134 Old Kingdom or Pyramid
Age: Dynasties 3–6 (*First great
flowering of Egyptian culture*)
*c.*2134–2040 1st Intermediate Period:
Dynasties 7–11

2nd millennium BC
*c.*2040–1786 Middle Kingdom: Dynasties
11–12 (*Second great age of Egyptian
culture*)
*c.*1786–1540 2nd Intermediate Period:
Dynasties 13–17 (*including Hyksos*)
*c.*1552–1069 New Kingdom or Empire:
Dynasties 18–20 (*Third great period
in Egyptian civilization*)
1552–1305 (or 1294) 18th Dynasty
(selected reigns):
1490–1437 (or 1479–1426)
Tuthmosis III
1390–1353 (or 1394–1357)
Amenophis III
1361–1345 (or 1365–1349)
Amenophis IV/Akhenaten
1305–1198 (or 1294–1187) 19th Dynasty
(selected reigns):
1305–1304 (or 1294–1293) Rameses I
1304–1290 (or 1293–1279) Sethos I
1290–1224 (or 1279–1213) Rameses II
1224–1214 (or 1213–1203) Merenptah
1198–1069 (or 1187–1069) 20th Dynasty
(*i.e.* Setnakht and Rameses III–XI)

1st millennium BC
*c.*1069–332 Late Period: Dynasties 21–31
*Long period of decay interspersed with
occasional brief periods of recovery*
(selected reigns):
945–715 22nd Dynasty
945–924 Shoshenq I (Shishak)
716–664 25th Dynasty
690–664 Taharqa ('Tirhakah')
664–525 26th Dynasty
664–656 Tanwetamani ('Tanutamen')
664–610 Psammeticus I
610–595 Neco II
595–589 Psammeticus II
589–570 Apries (Hophra)
*c.*332–30 Hellenistic Period
*c.*332–323 Alexander the Great

Old Testament History

1. FROM ABRAHAM TO SAUL
(There are two possible sets of dates for this early period.)

Higher chronology	Lower chronology	
c.2165–1990 BC	c.2000–1825 BC	Abraham
c.2065–1885	c.1900–1720	Isaac
c.2000–1860	c.1840–1700	Jacob
c.1910–1800	c.1750–1640	Joseph
c.1875	c.1700	Entry into Egypt
c.1450	c.1260	Exodus
c.1380–1050	c.1200–1050	Judges period

2. THE MONARCHY
a. 1050 (or 1045)–931/930 BC The United Monarchy

1050 (or 1045)–1011/10	Saul
1011/10–971/70	David
971/70–931/30	Solomon

b. 931/30–587 The Divided Monarchy

JUDAH

931/30–913 Rehoboam
  925 Sheshonq invades Palestine
913–911/10 Abijam
911/10–870/69 Asa
870/69–848 Jehoshaphat (co-regent 873/72)
848–841 Jehoram (co-regent from 853)
841 Ahaziah
841–835 Athaliah
835–796 Joash
796–767 Amaziah
767–740/39 Azariah (Uzziah) (co-regent from 791/90)
740/39–732/31 Jotham (co-regent from 750)
732/31–716/15 Ahaz (co-regent from 744/43; senior partner from 735)
716/15–687/86 Hezekiah
687/86–642/41 Manasseh (co-regent from 696/95)
642/41–640/39 Amon
640/39–609 Josiah
609 Jehoahaz
609–597 Jehoiakim
  605 Battle of Carchemish. Daniel and his friends are taken to Babylon
597 Jehoiachin
  597 2 Adar (15/16 March) Jerusalem taken by Nebuchadrezzar II. Many Jews exiled to Babylon including Jehoiachin and Ezekiel
597–587 Zedekiah
  587 Fall of Jerusalem. More Jews into exile in Babylon

ISRAEL

931/30–910/09 Jeroboam I
910/09–909/08 Nadab
909/08–886/85 Baasha
886/85–885/84 Elah
885/84 Zimri
885/84 Tibni
885/84–874/73 Omri
874/73–853 Ahab
853–852 Ahaziah
852–841 Joram
841–814/13 Jehu
814/13–798 Jehoahaz
798–782/81 Jehoash
782/81–753 Jeroboam II (co-regent from 793/92)
753–752 Zechariah
752 Shallum
752–742/41 Menahem
742/41–740/39 Pekahiah
740/39–732/31 Pekah
732/31–723/22 Hoshea
  722 Fall of Samaria

3. AFTER THE EXILE

539 Babylon falls to Cyrus, king of Persia. Jews return to rebuild the Temple
538 Zerubbabel, Sheshbazzar and others return to Jerusalem
537 Rebuilding of the Temple begun
520 Temple-building resumed
516 Temple completed 3 Adar (10 March)
458 Ezra goes to Jerusalem
445–433 Nehemiah at Jerusalem
332 Palestine comes under the control of Alexander the Great

ACKNOWLEDGMENTS

The following sources are acknowledged for the illustrations which appear throughout the book (credits given by page number):

Page 13: *New Bible Dictionary*, London: IVP 1962, p178.
Page 15: *New Bible Dictionary*, 2nd edition, Leicester: IVP 1982, p158.
Page 54: *Biblical Archaeology Review*, Washington DC: Biblical Archaeology Society. Vol IX, no 5: Sept/Oct 1983, p49. (Subscriptions to *BAR* are available by writing to the Biblical Archaeological Society, 3000 Conneticut Avenue, NW, Suite 300, Washington DC 20008, USA.
Page 65: *Biblical Archaeology Review*. Vol X, no 2: March/April 1984, p68.
Page 68: D Ussishkin, *The Conquest of Lachish by Sennacherib*, Tel Aviv: Tel Aviv University Institute of Archaeology 1982, p31.
Page 71: *Excavations in the Negev: Beersheba and Tel Masos*, Tel Aviv: Tel Aviv University Institute of Archaeology 1974, p8. Adapted from *Illustrated Bible Dictionary*, Leicester: IVP 1980.
Pages 94, 97, 98, 99: Adapted from *Biblical Archaeology Review*. Vol VI, no 2: March/April 1980, pp11–22.
Page 95: B Mazar et al, *Jerusalem Revealed*, Jerusalem: Israel Exploration Society 1975, p5.
Page 113: D Ussishkin, *The Conquest of Lachish by Sennacherib*, p122.
Page 115: Y Yadin, *The art of warfare in biblical lands in the light of archaeological discovery*, London: Weidenfeld and Nicolson, 1963.
Page 129 The Seal of Shema: A Parrot, *Samaria, the capital of the Kingdom of Israel*, London: SCM 1958, p76; from H Gressmann, AOB.
Page 140: A Parrot, *Samaria, the capital of the Kingdom of Israel*, p74; from HES p239.
Page 145: *Tel Aviv*, Vol 4, nos 1–2: 1977, p5.
Page 150: *Illustrated Bible Dictionary*, Leicester: IVP 1980, p1527.
Pages 158 and 159: Time charts adapted from *New Bible Atlas*, Leicester: IVP 1985, p116.

The drawings by C Davey on pages 54 and 56 are used by kind permission of the Editor of *Buried History*, the journal of the Australian Institute of Archaeology, Melbourne. **Page 54:** *Buried History* Vol 19 no 4: Dec 1983, p 58. **Page 56:** Vol 13 no 1: March 1977, p34.

The seals on pages 129 (the Seal of Yehozerah) and 135 are reproduced by kind permission of the Editor of the *Israel Exploration Journal*, the journal of the Israel Exploration Society, Jerusalem. **Page 129:** Vol 24, 1974, p27. **Page 135:** Vol 30, 1980, p171.

The illustration on **page 147** is taken by Y Yadin, *Hazor*, London 1975, Weidenfeld and Nicolson, p168, and is reproduced by kind permission of the publishers.

Subject Index

Scripture Index

*